TypeScript in Action: Building Modern Web Applications with TypeScript

Kameron Hussain and Frahaan Hussain

Published by Sonar Publishing, 2023.

While every precaution has been taken in the preparation of this book, the publisher assumes no responsibility for errors or omissions, or for damages resulting from the use of the information contained herein.

TYPESCRIPT IN ACTION: BUILDING MODERN WEB APPLICATIONS WITH TYPESCRIPT

First edition. November 13, 2023.

Copyright © 2023 Kameron Hussain and Frahaan Hussain.

ISBN: 979-8223861133

Written by Kameron Hussain and Frahaan Hussain.

Table of Contents

Chapter 10: Consuming APIs and Web Services

Example Authentication Implementation

Conclusion

Section 13.3: Authorization and Role-Based Access Control

Understanding Authorization

Implementing Authorization in TypeScript

Conclusion

Section 13.4: OAuth and OpenID Connect with TypeScript

Understanding OAuth and OpenID Connect

Integrating OAuth and OpenID Connect

Example OAuth Flow (Express.js)

Conclusion

Section 13.5: Securing Your Web Applications

1. Input Validation

2. Authentication and Authorization

3. Session Management

4. HTTPS

5. Content Security Policy (CSP)

6. Cross-Site Request Forgery (CSRF) Protection

7. Security Headers

8. Broken Access Control

9. Security Headers

10. Denial of Service (DoS) and Distributed Denial of Service (DDoS) Attacks

11. Security Patch Management

12. Security Education and Training

Section 18.2: Secure Coding Practices in TypeScript

1. Input Validation and Sanitization

2. Use Parameterized Queries

3. Avoid Eval and Unsafe Reflection

4. Authentication and Authorization

5. Prevent Information Leakage

6. Use Security Libraries

7. Data Encryption

8. Regular Code Audits and Security Scans

Section 18.3: Cross-Site Scripting (XSS) Prevention

1. Input Validation and Output Encoding

2. Content Security Policy (CSP)

3. Use DOM Manipulation Libraries Safely

4. Sanitize HTML

5. Avoid innerHTML

6. Keep Dependencies Updated

7. Security Testing

Section 18.4: Cross-Site Request Forgery (CSRF) Protection

1. Use Anti-CSRF Tokens

2. SameSite Cookies

3. Validate Referrer Header

4. Use HTTP Methods Safely

5. Implement Reauthentication

Section 18.5: Security Auditing and Vulnerability Scanning

1. Code Reviews

2. Penetration Testing

3. Dependency Scanning

4. Security Headers

5. Security Patch Management

6. Security Training and Awareness

1. Progressive Web Apps (PWAs)

2. Serverless Architecture

3. Jamstack Architecture

4. WebAssembly (Wasm)

5. Single Page Applications (SPAs)

6. Micro Frontends

7. Web3 and Blockchain

8. Conclusion

Section 20.3: TypeScript and WebAssembly

WebAssembly and TypeScript

Benefits of Using TypeScript with WebAssembly

Example: Using TypeScript with a WebAssembly Module

Conclusion

ASSISTANT

Section 20.3: TypeScript and WebAssembly

WebAssembly and Its Benefits

Integrating TypeScript with WebAssembly

Example Use Cases

TypeScript and WebAssembly Tooling

Conclusion

Section 20.4: Progressive Enhancement with TypeScript

Core Principles of Progressive Enhancement

TypeScript's Role in Progressive Enhancement

Practical Implementation

TypeScript and Feature Detection

Conclusion

Section 20.5: Keeping Up with TypeScript Updates

1. Official TypeScript Website

2. TypeScript Release Notes

3. TypeScript's npm Package

4. Visual Studio Code Integration

5. Community and Forums

Updating Your TypeScript Projects

Chapter 1: Introduction to TypeScript

1.1 What is TypeScript?

TypeScript is a statically typed superset of JavaScript that adds type annotations and other features to the language. It was developed by Microsoft and has gained popularity among developers for its ability to catch type-related errors at compile-time, improving code quality and maintainability.

TypeScript's Key Features

Here are some of the key features of TypeScript:

1. **Static Typing**: TypeScript introduces static typing, allowing you to specify the types of variables, function parameters, and return values. This helps catch type-related errors early in the development process.
2. **Enhanced Tooling**: TypeScript comes with rich tooling support, including code editors like Visual Studio Code that offer auto-completion, type checking, and refactoring capabilities.
3. **Modern JavaScript Features**: TypeScript supports the latest ECMAScript features, making it a powerful choice for modern web development.
4. **Compatibility**: TypeScript is designed to be compatible with existing JavaScript code, so you can gradually adopt it in your projects.
5. **Type Inference**: TypeScript can infer types when they are not explicitly specified, reducing the need for verbose type annotations.

Why Use TypeScript?

There are several benefits to using TypeScript:

- **Type Safety**: TypeScript helps catch type errors during development, reducing the likelihood of runtime errors in production.

- **Code Quality**: With TypeScript's static typing, code becomes more self-documenting and easier to understand.

- **Enhanced Productivity**: TypeScript's tooling and type checking features can improve developer productivity by providing real-time feedback.

- **Large Codebases**: TypeScript is particularly useful for large codebases where maintaining code quality is crucial.

Installing TypeScript

To get started with TypeScript, you need to install it globally using npm (Node Package Manager):

npm install -g typescript

After installation, you can use the tsc command to compile TypeScript code into JavaScript.

TypeScript vs. JavaScript

It's important to note that TypeScript is not a replacement for JavaScript but rather a superset of it. You can use TypeScript alongside JavaScript in your projects. JavaScript code is valid

TypeScript code, which means you can gradually adopt TypeScript in existing projects.

In the next sections of this chapter, we will explore how to set up your development environment for TypeScript and dive deeper into TypeScript's relationship with JavaScript.

Stay tuned for more in-depth discussions and hands-on examples throughout this book as we explore the various aspects of TypeScript and how it can enhance your web development experience.

1.2 Benefits of Using TypeScript

TypeScript offers several significant benefits that make it a compelling choice for web developers. In this section, we'll explore some of the key advantages of using TypeScript in your projects.

1. Type Safety

One of the primary benefits of TypeScript is its strong static typing system. By specifying types for variables, function parameters, and return values, TypeScript helps catch type-related errors at compile-time. This means you can identify and fix issues before running your code, reducing the likelihood of runtime errors in production. Type safety is especially valuable in large and complex codebases, where it can be challenging to keep track of data types.

2. Improved Code Quality

TypeScript promotes better code quality by making your codebase more self-documenting. With type annotations, it's easier to understand the intended usage of functions and variables. This enhanced readability not only benefits you as the developer but also makes your code more maintainable for your team members or collaborators. It leads to fewer misunderstandings about how certain parts of the code should work.

3. Enhanced Tooling

TypeScript comes with a rich set of development tools that can significantly improve your productivity. Popular code editors like Visual Studio Code provide features like auto-completion, real-time error checking, and intelligent code navigation when working with TypeScript. These tools streamline the development process and help you write more reliable code faster.

4. Modern JavaScript Features

TypeScript is designed to support the latest ECMAScript (ES) features. This means you can take advantage of the most recent JavaScript enhancements, such as async/await, destructuring, and arrow functions, while still enjoying the benefits of static typing. This allows you to write cleaner and more concise code without sacrificing type safety.

5. Compatibility with JavaScript

One of TypeScript's strengths is its compatibility with existing JavaScript code. You can gradually introduce TypeScript into your projects by renaming JavaScript files to .ts files and adding type annotations incrementally. This flexibility means you don't need to rewrite your entire codebase to start benefiting from TypeScript.

6. Strong Community and Ecosystem

TypeScript has gained a robust and active community of developers who contribute to its growth and provide a wealth of resources and libraries. This vibrant ecosystem includes type definitions for popular JavaScript libraries, frameworks, and tools, making it easier to incorporate TypeScript into a wide range of projects.

7. Investment in Long-Term Maintainability

Using TypeScript is an investment in the long-term maintainability of your projects. By reducing the likelihood of type-related bugs and making your codebase more readable and self-explanatory, TypeScript helps ensure that your code remains manageable and extensible as your application evolves.

8. Learning and Career Growth

Learning TypeScript can be a valuable skill for your career as a web developer. Many companies are adopting TypeScript for their front-end and back-end development, and having proficiency in TypeScript can make you a more attractive candidate in the job market. It's a skill that aligns well with the industry's shift toward statically typed languages.

In summary, TypeScript offers a range of benefits, including type safety, improved code quality, enhanced tooling, support for modern JavaScript features, compatibility with JavaScript, a strong community, long-term maintainability, and career growth opportunities. These advantages make TypeScript a compelling choice for web developers looking to build robust and maintainable applications.

1.3 Setting Up Your Development Environment

Before you can start working with TypeScript, you'll need to set up your development environment. In this section, we'll walk you through the steps to get TypeScript up and running on your computer.

1. Installing Node.js and npm

TypeScript relies on Node.js and npm (Node Package Manager) for development and package management. If you don't already have them installed, follow these steps:

1. **Download Node.js**: Visit the Node.js official website[1] and download the LTS (Long-Term Support) version for your operating system. LTS versions are recommended for most users as they offer stability and security updates.
2. **Install Node.js**: Run the installer you downloaded and follow the installation instructions for your operating system. After installation, you should have both Node.js and npm available on your system.
3. **Verify Installation**: Open a command prompt or terminal window and run the following commands to verify that Node.js and npm are installed:

```
node -v
```

```
npm -v
```

These commands should display the installed Node.js and npm versions, confirming that the installation was successful.

---

1. https://nodejs.org/

2. Installing TypeScript Globally

Once you have Node.js and npm installed, you can install TypeScript globally using npm. Open your command prompt or terminal and run the following command:

npm install -g typescript

This command installs TypeScript globally on your system, making the tsc (TypeScript Compiler) command available.

3. Creating a TypeScript Project

Now that you have TypeScript installed, let's create a simple TypeScript project. Here are the steps:

1. **Create a Project Folder**: Create a new directory for your TypeScript project. You can do this using your file explorer or with the following command:

mkdir my-ts-project

1. **Navigate to the Project Folder**: Change your working directory to the newly created project folder:

cd my-ts-project

1. **Initialize a TypeScript Project**: Run the following command to initialize a TypeScript project. This command will create a tsconfig.json file, which is used to configure TypeScript settings for your project:

tsc—init

1. **Edit tsconfig.json**: Open the tsconfig.json file in a code

editor of your choice. This file allows you to specify TypeScript compiler options and configure your project. You can adjust settings according to your project requirements.

4. Writing and Compiling TypeScript Code

With your TypeScript project set up, you can now start writing TypeScript code in .ts files. Here's a simple example:

Create a file named app.ts in your project folder and add the following TypeScript code:

```typescript
function greet(name: string): string {

return `Hello, ${name}!`;

}

const message = greet("John");

console.log(message);
```

This code defines a function greet that takes a name parameter and returns a greeting message. It then calls the function and logs the result to the console.

To compile this TypeScript code into JavaScript, open your command prompt or terminal and run the following command from your project folder:

```
tsc
```

This will use the TypeScript compiler to transpile your app.ts file into a corresponding app.js file.

5. Running TypeScript Code

Now that you've compiled your TypeScript code into JavaScript, you can run it using Node.js. In your command prompt or terminal, execute the following command:

node app.js

You should see the output of your TypeScript program, which in this case will be the greeting message logged to the console.

Congratulations! You've successfully set up your development environment for TypeScript and written and executed your first TypeScript program. You're now ready to explore more TypeScript features and build web applications with confidence.

1.4 TypeScript's Relationship with JavaScript

Understanding TypeScript's relationship with JavaScript is crucial when working with TypeScript. TypeScript builds upon JavaScript and is designed to be fully compatible with it. In this section, we'll explore the key aspects of this relationship.

1. TypeScript is a Superset of JavaScript

TypeScript is often referred to as a "superset" of JavaScript. This means that any valid JavaScript code is also valid TypeScript code. You can take existing JavaScript code and gradually add TypeScript features to it without needing to rewrite everything.

For example, consider a simple JavaScript function:

```
function greet(name) {
return "Hello, " + name + "!";
```

```
}
```

```
console.log(greet("John"));
```

This JavaScript code is entirely valid in TypeScript. However, you can enhance it with TypeScript's static typing capabilities by adding type annotations:

```
function greet(name: string): string {

return `Hello, ${name}!`;

}

console.log(greet("John"));
```

By adding type annotations, you make your code more robust and self-documenting without altering its JavaScript functionality.

2. TypeScript Compiles to JavaScript

When you write TypeScript code, it's essential to understand that TypeScript itself doesn't run in browsers or Node.js directly. Instead, TypeScript code is compiled into plain JavaScript code, which is executed by the runtime environment.

The TypeScript compiler (tsc) processes your TypeScript files and generates equivalent JavaScript files. This compilation step ensures that your TypeScript code is compatible with all JavaScript environments.

3. ECMAScript Compatibility

TypeScript is designed to align closely with ECMAScript (ES) standards. This means that TypeScript supports the latest features introduced in JavaScript. As a developer, you can leverage modern

JavaScript syntax and features while enjoying TypeScript's additional benefits, such as static typing.

For instance, you can use ES6 features like arrow functions, template literals, destructuring, and more in TypeScript:

const numbers = [1, 2, 3, 4, 5];

const doubled = numbers.map((n) => n * 2);

console.log(doubled); // [2, 4, 6, 8, 10]

4. JavaScript Libraries and Frameworks

TypeScript can be seamlessly integrated with popular JavaScript libraries and frameworks. Many libraries provide TypeScript type definitions that enable type checking and auto-completion when using them in TypeScript projects. This compatibility extends to front-end libraries like React, Angular, and Vue.js, as well as back-end frameworks like Express.js.

To use TypeScript with JavaScript libraries and frameworks, you typically need to install the respective type definition packages using npm. These packages provide TypeScript with the necessary type information to ensure type safety and code completion when interacting with the library's APIs.

5. Transitioning to TypeScript

If you're already working on a JavaScript project and want to introduce TypeScript gradually, you can follow a few steps:

1. Rename your existing .js files to .ts files. TypeScript will recognize and compile them.
2. Start adding type annotations to your functions, variables,

and other code as needed.

3. Use TypeScript features incrementally, such as interfaces, classes, and advanced type checking, when they provide value to your project.
4. Install type definition packages for JavaScript libraries you're using to benefit from TypeScript's type checking.

By transitioning your project in this way, you can experience the advantages of TypeScript while maintaining backward compatibility with your existing JavaScript code.

In summary, TypeScript is a superset of JavaScript, and it maintains compatibility with JavaScript throughout its development process. TypeScript code is compiled to JavaScript, ensuring that it can run in any JavaScript environment. Additionally, TypeScript aligns closely with ECMAScript standards and supports modern JavaScript features. It can be smoothly integrated with JavaScript libraries and frameworks, making it a versatile choice for web development projects.

1.5 TypeScript Tooling and Editors

TypeScript offers a rich ecosystem of tools and editors that can significantly enhance your development experience. In this section, we'll explore some of the essential tools and editors you can use when working with TypeScript.

1. TypeScript Compiler (tsc)

The TypeScript compiler, often referred to as tsc, is a fundamental tool for working with TypeScript. It's responsible for transpiling TypeScript code into JavaScript, making it executable in various JavaScript environments.

To compile a TypeScript file, you can use the following command:

tsc your-file.ts

By running this command, TypeScript will generate a corresponding JavaScript file, such as your-file.js. You can then execute the JavaScript code in your preferred runtime environment.

2. Visual Studio Code (VS Code)

Visual Studio Code is a popular code editor developed by Microsoft that offers exceptional support for TypeScript. VS Code provides features like intelligent code completion, real-time error checking, and automatic TypeScript compilation. It's an excellent choice for TypeScript development.

To get started with TypeScript in VS Code, follow these steps:

1. Install Visual Studio Code from the official website[2].
2. Install the "TypeScript and JavaScript Language Features" extension by Microsoft. You can search for it in the VS Code extensions marketplace and install it.
3. Open your TypeScript project folder in VS Code, and you'll benefit from TypeScript-specific features like type checking and code navigation.

3. TypeScript Playground

The TypeScript Playground[3] is an online tool provided by the TypeScript team. It allows you to write, experiment with, and share TypeScript code directly in your web browser. The TypeScript Playground provides instant feedback on type checking and

---

2. https://code.visualstudio.com/

3. https://www.typescriptlang.org/play

compiles your code on the fly, making it a valuable resource for learning and prototyping.

4. tsconfig.json

The tsconfig.json file is a configuration file that allows you to specify TypeScript compiler options and project settings. It plays a crucial role in controlling how TypeScript compiles your code. You can define options like the target ECMAScript version, module system, and code organization in this file.

Here's a minimal tsconfig.json example:

```
{

"compilerOptions": {

"target": "ES6",

"module": "CommonJS",

"outDir": "./dist"

},

"include": ["src/**/*.ts"],

"exclude": ["node_modules"]

}
```

5. TypeScript Declaration Files (*.d.ts)

Declaration files, often denoted with a .d.ts extension, provide type information for JavaScript libraries and modules that were not originally written in TypeScript. These files enable TypeScript to perform type checking and provide autocompletion when using third-party JavaScript code.

You can find many declaration files for popular libraries on the DefinitelyTyped repository or install them using npm.

6. Type Checking

TypeScript's primary feature is static type checking, which helps catch type-related errors during development. When you write TypeScript code in a compatible editor like Visual Studio Code, you'll receive real-time feedback about potential type issues as you write your code. This immediate feedback enhances code quality and reduces the likelihood of runtime errors.

7. Code Navigation

TypeScript-aware editors like VS Code provide excellent code navigation capabilities. You can easily jump to the definition of a variable, function, or class by clicking on it. This feature simplifies code exploration and debugging, especially in larger codebases.

8. Refactoring Support

Refactoring is an essential part of code maintenance and improvement. TypeScript editors often offer built-in refactoring tools that help you rename variables, extract functions, and perform other code transformations safely and efficiently.

In summary, TypeScript offers a range of tools and editors that enhance your development experience. The TypeScript compiler (tsc) is responsible for transpiling TypeScript to JavaScript, while Visual Studio Code provides an exceptional TypeScript development environment. The TypeScript Playground is a web-based tool for experimentation, and the tsconfig.json file allows you to configure your TypeScript projects. Declaration files and type checking ensure compatibility with JavaScript libraries, while code navigation and refactoring support help streamline development and maintenance tasks. Leveraging these tools and editors can make your TypeScript development workflow efficient and productive.

Chapter 2: Getting Started with TypeScript

2.1 Installing TypeScript

Before you can start working with TypeScript, you need to install it on your development machine. TypeScript can be installed globally using Node Package Manager (npm), which is a package manager commonly used for JavaScript and TypeScript development. In this section, we'll walk you through the steps to install TypeScript.

1. Prerequisites

Before you proceed with the installation, ensure that you have Node.js and npm (Node Package Manager) installed on your computer. You can download and install Node.js from the official website (https://nodejs.org/). npm is typically included with Node.js, so you don't need to install it separately.

2. Installing TypeScript

Once you have Node.js and npm installed, you can install TypeScript globally by running a simple npm command. Open your command prompt or terminal and enter the following command:

npm install -g typescript

- npm install is the command to install packages using npm.

- -g stands for "global," which means TypeScript will be installed globally on your system, making it accessible from any directory.

3. Verifying the Installation

After the installation is complete, you can verify that TypeScript is installed correctly by running the following commands in your command prompt or terminal:

tsc -v

This command will display the installed TypeScript version. If you see the TypeScript version number, it means TypeScript is successfully installed on your machine.

4. Updating TypeScript

TypeScript is regularly updated to include new features and bug fixes. To update TypeScript to the latest version, you can use the following npm command:

npm update -g typescript

This command will check for updates to the TypeScript package and install the latest version if available.

5. Understanding the tsc Command

The tsc command is the TypeScript compiler. You will use it to transpile TypeScript code into JavaScript. To compile a TypeScript file, simply navigate to the directory containing your TypeScript file and run:

tsc your-file.ts

This command will generate a JavaScript file with the same name as your TypeScript file but with the .js extension.

6. Uninstalling TypeScript

If you ever need to uninstall TypeScript, you can do so by running the following npm command:

npm uninstall -g typescript

This will remove TypeScript from your system.

In summary, installing TypeScript is a straightforward process. You need Node.js and npm installed, and then you can use npm to install TypeScript globally. After installation, you can verify the TypeScript version using the tsc -v command. Updating TypeScript to the latest version and uninstalling it can also be done with npm commands. With TypeScript successfully installed, you're ready to start writing and compiling TypeScript code in your development environment.

2.2 Your First TypeScript Program

Now that you have TypeScript installed, it's time to create your first TypeScript program. In this section, we'll walk you through the process of creating a simple TypeScript file, writing TypeScript code, and compiling it into JavaScript.

1. Creating a TypeScript File

To get started, open your text editor or integrated development environment (IDE) of choice. Create a new file with a .ts extension. This extension indicates that the file contains TypeScript code.

For example, you can create a file named hello.ts.

2. Writing TypeScript Code

In your hello.ts file, you can write your first TypeScript code. Let's start with a basic example:

```typescript
function sayHello(name: string) {

console.log(`Hello, ${name}!`);

}

const userName = "John";

sayHello(userName);
```

In this code snippet:

- We define a function sayHello that takes a parameter name of type string.

- Inside the function, we use a template string to log a greeting message to the console, including the provided name.

- We declare a constant userName with the value "John."

- Finally, we call the sayHello function, passing userName as an argument.

3. Compiling TypeScript to JavaScript

To compile your TypeScript code into JavaScript, you'll need to use the TypeScript compiler (tsc). Open your command prompt or terminal, navigate to the directory where your hello.ts file is located, and run the following command:

```
tsc hello.ts
```

This command will transpile your hello.ts file into JavaScript and generate a corresponding hello.js file in the same directory.

4. Running the JavaScript Code

Now that you have the hello.js file, you can run it using Node.js, as JavaScript is executed in the Node.js runtime. In your command prompt or terminal, run the following command:

node hello.js

You should see the output in the console:

Hello, John!

Congratulations! You've successfully created and executed your first TypeScript program. You wrote TypeScript code, compiled it into JavaScript, and ran it using Node.js.

5. TypeScript Features

In this simple example, you can already see one of TypeScript's key features in action: static typing. We specified that the name parameter of the sayHello function should be of type string. TypeScript checks types at compile-time, which helps catch potential type-related errors before running the code.

As you explore TypeScript further, you'll discover more advanced features, such as interfaces, classes, and powerful type inference. TypeScript provides a robust and expressive type system that can improve code quality and maintainability, especially in larger projects.

In the upcoming sections of this book, we'll delve deeper into TypeScript's features and explore how to use them effectively in various scenarios.

2.3 Basic Types in TypeScript

In TypeScript, you can work with a variety of basic data types to represent different kinds of values. These types help you specify the shape of your data and enable TypeScript to catch type-related errors during compilation. In this section, we'll explore some of the fundamental data types available in TypeScript.

1. Boolean

The boolean type represents true or false values. You can use it to declare variables that hold Boolean values. For example:

```
let isDone: boolean = false;
```

2. Number

The number type is used to represent numeric values, including integers and floating-point numbers. For instance:

```
let age: number = 30;
```

```
let price: number = 49.99;
```

3. String

The string type represents textual data, such as words, sentences, or characters. You can declare string variables like this:

```
let firstName: string = "John";
```

```
let greeting: string = `Hello, ${firstName}!`;
```

4. Array

An array is a data structure that can hold multiple values of the same or different types. You can specify the type of elements in an array using square brackets followed by the element type. Here's an example of an array of numbers:

let numbers: number[] = [1, 2, 3, 4, 5];

You can also use the Array generic type to define arrays:

let colors: Array<string> = ["red", "green", "blue"];

5. Tuple

A tuple is a fixed-size array where each element can have a different type. You declare a tuple by specifying the types for each element in square brackets. For example:

let person: [string, number] = ["John", 30];

6. Enum

An enum is a way to define a set of named constants. It's often used to represent a finite set of related values. Here's an example:

enum Color {

Red,

Green,

Blue,

}

let chosenColor: Color = Color.Green;

In this example, Color is an enum with three values: Red, Green, and Blue. You can assign these values to variables of type Color.

7. Any

The any type allows you to work with values of any type, effectively opting out of TypeScript's type checking. While any provides flexibility, it's generally best to avoid it when possible because it loses the benefits of static typing. For example:

```
let data: any = 42;

data = "Hello, TypeScript!";
```

8. Void

The void type is used for functions that don't return any value. It's often used for functions that perform actions but don't produce results. For example:

```
function logMessage(message: string): void {

console.log(message);

}
```

9. Null and Undefined

The null and undefined types represent the absence of value. They are often used when a variable may not have a value. For example:

```
let name: string | null = null;

let age: number | undefined;
```

These are some of the basic types you can use in TypeScript to define variables and specify the types of values they can hold. TypeScript's strong static typing helps you catch type-related errors early in the development process, making your code more robust and maintainable. In practice, you'll often use these basic types as building blocks to create more complex data structures and models for your applications.

2.4 Type Annotations and Inference

TypeScript offers a powerful type system that allows you to specify types explicitly using type annotations or rely on type inference to determine types automatically. In this section, we'll explore both approaches and understand when to use them.

1. Type Annotations

Type annotations involve explicitly specifying the data type for a variable or a function parameter. You use a colon (:) followed by the type to provide the annotation. Here's an example of type annotations:

let age: number = 30;

let firstName: string = "John";

In the code above, we've annotated the age variable with the number type and the firstName variable with the string type.

Type annotations are particularly useful when:

- You want to provide clear documentation about the expected types in your code.

- You want to explicitly specify types for variables that TypeScript can't infer accurately.

2. Type Inference

Type inference is one of TypeScript's key features. It automatically determines the types of variables based on their initial values or how they are used in the code. You don't need to explicitly specify types in many cases because TypeScript can infer them. Here's an example:

let age = 30; *// TypeScript infers `age` as `number`*

let firstName = "John"; *// TypeScript infers `firstName` as `string`*

In this code, TypeScript infers the types of age and firstName based on their assigned values.

Type inference is helpful when:

- You want to write more concise code without explicitly specifying types for every variable.

- The type can be unambiguously determined from the context.

- You're working with complex type relationships and don't want to manage lengthy type annotations.

3. Type Annotations for Functions

You can also use type annotations for function parameters and return values to provide explicit type information. Here's an example:

```
function add(a: number, b: number): number {

return a + b;

}
```

In this function, we've annotated both parameters a and b as number, and we've indicated that the function returns a number. Type annotations for functions are valuable because they clarify the expected input and output types and help prevent type-related errors.

4. Type Inference for Functions

TypeScript can also infer the types of function parameters and return values when they are not explicitly annotated:

```
function multiply(x, y) {

return x * y; // TypeScript infers parameter types and return type

}
```

In this example, TypeScript infers the types of x and y based on the types of the values passed when calling the function.

5. Using Type Annotations with Objects

When working with objects, you can use type annotations to specify the types of object properties. Here's an example:

```
let person: { name: string; age: number } = {

name: "John",

age: 30,

};
```

In this case, we've provided a type annotation for the person object, specifying that it should have a name property of type string and an age property of type number.

6. Type Inference with Objects

TypeScript can also infer object types based on their structure:

```
let person = {

name: "John",

age: 30,

};
```

In this example, TypeScript infers the types for the person object properties based on their initial values.

7. When to Use Type Annotations vs. Type Inference

The choice between type annotations and type inference depends on your specific use case:

- Use type annotations when you want to provide clear and explicit type information or when TypeScript cannot infer types accurately.

- Use type inference when the types can be unambiguously determined from the context, or when you want to write more concise code.

In practice, you'll often use a combination of both type annotations and type inference to strike a balance between code clarity and brevity. TypeScript's type system is flexible and adaptable to different coding styles and requirements.

2.5 Compiling TypeScript Code

Compiling TypeScript code is a crucial step before you can run it in a JavaScript runtime environment. TypeScript code is written in .ts files and needs to be transformed into equivalent JavaScript code (.js) to be executed by browsers, Node.js, or other JavaScript environments. In this section, we'll explore how to compile TypeScript code using the TypeScript compiler (tsc) and various compilation options.

1. Basic Compilation

To compile a TypeScript file, you can use the following command:

tsc your-file.ts

This command instructs the TypeScript compiler to process your-file.ts and generate the corresponding JavaScript output in a file named your-file.js. You can then run the JavaScript code in a JavaScript runtime environment.

2. Compiling Multiple Files

If your project consists of multiple TypeScript files, you can compile them all at once by specifying the entry file or using a tsconfig.json configuration file. Here's an example of compiling multiple files:

tsc file1.ts file2.ts file3.ts

Alternatively, you can create a tsconfig.json file in your project's root directory to specify the compilation options and list the files to include. Here's a simple tsconfig.json file:

{

"files": ["file1.ts", "file2.ts", "file3.ts"]

}

Then, you can compile all the files in the configuration using:

tsc

3. Watching for Changes

To make the development process more convenient, you can use the —watch flag with the tsc command. This flag tells the TypeScript compiler to monitor your TypeScript files for changes and recompile them automatically when any changes are detected. For example:

tsc—watch your-file.ts

4. Configuration with tsconfig.json

A tsconfig.json file allows you to specify various compiler options and settings for your TypeScript project. By defining a tsconfig.json file, you can streamline the compilation process and ensure consistent settings across your project. Here's a basic tsconfig.json example:

{

"compilerOptions": {

"target": "ES6",

"outDir": "dist"

},

"include": ["src/**/*.ts"],

"exclude": ["node_modules"]

}

In this example:

- "compilerOptions" specify compiler settings like the ECMAScript target version and the output directory.

- "include" specifies which files or directories should be included for compilation.

- "exclude" specifies which files or directories should be excluded from compilation.

You can compile your TypeScript project using the tsc command without specifying individual files when a tsconfig.json file is present in the project directory:

tsc

5. Generating Source Maps

Source maps are useful for debugging TypeScript code in browsers or development tools. They allow you to map the JavaScript code back to the original TypeScript code, making debugging easier. To generate source maps during compilation, add the "sourceMap" option to your tsconfig.json file:

{

"compilerOptions": {

"sourceMap": **true**

}

}

With this option enabled, the TypeScript compiler will generate .js.map files alongside the compiled JavaScript files.

6. Strict Type Checking

TypeScript offers various strict type checking options that can help catch potential errors and enforce stricter type rules. Some of these options include "strictNullChecks", "strictFunctionTypes", and "noImplicitAny". You can configure them in your tsconfig.json file based on your project's requirements.

7. Custom Build Scripts

In larger projects or build pipelines, you might want to incorporate TypeScript compilation into custom build scripts or use build tools like Webpack, Gulp, or Grunt to automate the compilation process. These tools can help you manage complex build tasks and optimizations for your TypeScript projects.

In summary, compiling TypeScript code is an essential step in the development process. You can use the TypeScript compiler (tsc) to transform TypeScript code into JavaScript. You can compile individual files, multiple files, or an entire project using a tsconfig.json configuration file. Options in tsconfig.json allow you to customize compilation settings, enable strict type checking, generate source maps, and more. Automating the compilation process with build tools can be beneficial for larger projects. By mastering TypeScript compilation, you ensure your code is ready for execution in various JavaScript runtime environments.

Chapter 3: TypeScript Language Fundamentals

3.1 Variables and Constants

In TypeScript, variables and constants are used to store and manage data within your programs. Understanding how to declare and use them is fundamental to writing effective TypeScript code.

1. Declaring Variables

To declare a variable in TypeScript, you can use the let keyword, followed by the variable name and an optional type annotation. For example:

let age: number = 30;

let name: string = "John";

In this code, we've declared a variable age with the type number and a variable name with the type string. TypeScript's type system allows for strict type checking, ensuring that you can only assign values of the specified types to these variables.

2. Initializing Variables

You can also declare and initialize a variable in a single step. TypeScript will infer the variable's type based on the assigned value:

let age = 30; *// TypeScript infers `age` as `number`*

let name = "John"; *// TypeScript infers `name` as `string`*

In this case, TypeScript uses type inference to determine the types of age and name.

3. Constants with const

In addition to variables, TypeScript supports constants using the const keyword. Constants are variables whose values cannot be reassigned once they are set. Here's an example:

```typescript
const pi: number = 3.14159;
```

By declaring a constant with const, you ensure that its value remains unchanged throughout the program. Attempting to reassign a value to a constant will result in a compilation error.

4. Variable Scoping

Variables in TypeScript have scope, which determines where in the code the variable is accessible. The two main types of variable scope are:

- **Global Scope**: Variables declared outside of any functions or code blocks have global scope and can be accessed from anywhere in the program.

- **Local Scope**: Variables declared within a function or code block have local scope and are only accessible within that specific function or block.

Here's an example illustrating variable scope:

```typescript
let globalVariable = "I'm global"; // Global variable

function exampleFunction() {

let localVariable = "I'm local"; // Local variable

console.log(globalVariable); // Accessing the global variable

console.log(localVariable); // Accessing the local variable
```

```
}

exampleFunction();

console.log(globalVariable); // Accessing the global variable outside
the function

console.log(localVariable); // This will result in a compilation error
```

5. Hoisting

TypeScript, like JavaScript, exhibits variable hoisting behavior. This means that variable declarations are moved to the top of their containing function or block during compilation, regardless of where they are declared in the source code. However, the initializations (assignments) remain in place.

```
function hoistingExample() {

console.log(myVar); // Outputs: undefined

var myVar = "I am hoisted!";

console.log(myVar); // Outputs: I am hoisted!

}
```

In the example above, even though myVar is accessed before its declaration, it is hoisted to the top of the function's scope, resulting in undefined during the first console.log.

6. Block-Scoped Variables with let and const

To mitigate some of the issues associated with variable hoisting, TypeScript introduced the let and const keywords, which allow you to declare block-scoped variables. Block-scoped variables are only accessible within the block where they are defined, whether it's a function, loop, or code block.

```
function blockScopeExample() {

if (true) {

let blockScopedVar = "I am block-scoped!";

console.log(blockScopedVar); // Outputs: I am block-scoped!

}

console.log(blockScopedVar); // This will result in a compilation error

}
```

In this example, blockScopedVar is only accessible within the if block and not outside it.

7. Summary

In this section, you've learned about declaring and initializing variables and constants in TypeScript. You've seen how TypeScript provides type annotations to specify the data type of variables, and how type inference can determine types based on assigned values. You also explored the concepts of variable scope, hoisting, and block-scoped variables. Understanding these fundamentals is essential for effective TypeScript development, as variables and constants are the building blocks of your programs.

3.2 Functions in TypeScript

Functions are a fundamental part of any programming language, and TypeScript provides strong typing support for defining and using functions. In this section, we'll explore how to declare and work with functions in TypeScript, including specifying function signatures and parameter types.

1. Function Declarations

In TypeScript, you can declare functions using the function keyword, followed by the function name and a set of parentheses for parameters. Here's a simple function declaration:

```typescript
function greet(name: string): string {

return `Hello, ${name}!`;

}
```

In this example, we've declared a function named greet that takes a single parameter name of type string and returns a string. TypeScript allows you to specify parameter types and return types explicitly for functions, providing type safety.

2. Function Expressions

Functions can also be defined as expressions and assigned to variables. These are known as function expressions. Here's an example:

```typescript
const add = function (a: number, b: number): number {

return a + b;

};
```

In this code, we've defined an anonymous function and assigned it to the add variable. The function takes two parameters, a and b, both of type number, and returns a number. TypeScript can infer the function's type based on its structure, but you can also provide explicit type annotations as shown.

3. Arrow Functions

Arrow functions provide a concise way to define functions, especially when they have a single expression. Here's how you can declare an arrow function:

```typescript
const multiply = (a: number, b: number): number => a * b;
```

In this example, the multiply function takes two parameters, a and b, both of type number, and returns their product as a number. Arrow functions automatically capture the surrounding this context, making them suitable for certain use cases like callbacks.

4. Optional Parameters

In TypeScript, you can make function parameters optional by appending a ? to their names in the parameter list. Optional parameters allow you to call a function without providing values for those parameters. Here's an example:

```typescript
function sendMessage(message: string, recipient?: string): void {

if (recipient) {

console.log(`Message to ${recipient}: ${message}`);

} else {

console.log(`Message: ${message}`);

}

}
```

```typescript
sendMessage("Hello"); // Outputs: Message: Hello
```

```typescript
sendMessage("Hi", "Alice"); // Outputs: Message to Alice: Hi
```

In this code, the recipient parameter is optional. When calling the sendMessage function without providing a recipient, it defaults to undefined. You can check if a value is provided before using it within the function.

5. Default Parameter Values

You can also specify default values for parameters using the assignment operator (=). When you don't provide a value for a parameter, it takes the default value. Here's an example:

```typescript
function greetUser(name: string = "Guest"): string {

return `Hello, ${name}!`;

}
```

```typescript
console.log(greetUser()); // Outputs: Hello, Guest!
```

```typescript
console.log(greetUser("Alice")); // Outputs: Hello, Alice!
```

In this code, the name parameter has a default value of "Guest". If you don't provide a value when calling greetUser, it uses the default value. You can still override the default by passing a different value.

6. Rest Parameters

Rest parameters allow you to pass a variable number of arguments to a function. They are denoted by three dots (...) followed by a parameter name. Rest parameters collect all the remaining arguments into an array. Here's an example:

```typescript
function sum(...numbers: number[]): number {
```

```typescript
return numbers.reduce((total, num) => total + num, 0);

}

console.log(sum(1, 2, 3)); // Outputs: 6

console.log(sum(10, 20, 30, 40)); // Outputs: 100
```

In this code, the sum function accepts any number of numbers as arguments and returns their sum. Rest parameters are useful when you need to handle functions with a variable number of arguments.

7. Function Overloading

Function overloading allows you to define multiple function signatures for a single function, each with a different set of parameter types and return types. TypeScript uses the function signature to determine which overload to use based on the arguments provided. Here's an example:

```typescript
function greetUser(name: string): string;

function greetUser(firstName: string, lastName: string): string;

function greetUser(arg1: string, arg2?: string): string {

if (arg2) {

return `Hello, ${arg1} ${arg2}!`;

} else {

return `Hello, ${arg1}!`;

}

}
```

console.log(greetUser("Alice")); *// Outputs: Hello, Alice!*

console.log(greetUser("John", "Doe")); *// Outputs: Hello, John Doe!*

In this code, we have two function signatures for greetUser: one that takes a single name parameter and another that takes two parameters, firstName and lastName. The actual implementation of the function follows these signatures. TypeScript determines the appropriate signature to use based on the number and types of arguments provided during the function call.

8. Function Types

Functions in TypeScript can be treated as values and have types just like other data. You can specify function types when declaring variables or function parameters. Here's an example:

type MathOperation = (a: number, b: number) => number;

const add: MathOperation = (a, b) => a + b;

const subtract: MathOperation = (a, b) => a - b;

In this code, we've defined a MathOperation type that represents a function taking two number parameters and returning a number. We then declare variables add and subtract with the MathOperation type and provide arrow function implementations.

9. Callback Functions

Callback functions are commonly used in asynchronous programming. You can specify the type of a callback function using function types. Here's an example using a callback to simulate asynchronous operations:

function fetchData(callback: (data: string) => void): void {

```typescript
setTimeout(() => {

const data = "This is the fetched data.";

callback(data);

}, 1000);

}

fetchData((result) => {

console.log(`Fetched data: ${result}`);

});
```

##

3.3 Interfaces and Types

Interfaces and types are essential concepts in TypeScript that help you define the shape and structure of objects and other data structures. They provide a way to enforce a contract for the structure of an object, ensuring that it adheres to a specific shape. In this section, we'll explore both interfaces and type aliases and how they are used in TypeScript.

1. Interfaces

Interfaces are a core feature of TypeScript and allow you to define the structure of an object, including its properties and their types. You can then use these interfaces to enforce that objects conform to a specific shape. Here's an example of defining an interface and using it:

```typescript
```

```typescript
interface Person {

firstName: string;

lastName: string;

age: number;

}

function greet(person: Person): string {

return `Hello, ${person.firstName} ${person.lastName}!`;

}

const alice: Person = {

firstName: "Alice",

lastName: "Johnson",

age: 30,

};

console.log(greet(alice)); // Outputs: Hello, Alice Johnson!
```

In this code, we've defined an interface Person with properties firstName, lastName, and age. The greet function takes an argument of type Person, ensuring that it receives an object with the expected properties.

2. Optional Properties in Interfaces

You can make properties in an interface optional by using the ? modifier. This means that objects implementing the interface can omit those properties if needed. Here's an example:

```typescript
interface User {

username: string;

email: string;

age?: number; // Optional property

}

const newUser: User = {

username: "john_doe",

email: "john@example.com",

};

console.log(newUser); // Outputs: { username: 'john_doe', email: 'john@example.com' }
```

In this case, the age property is optional in the User interface, allowing objects to be created without specifying it.

3. Readonly Properties

You can make properties readonly in an interface using the readonly modifier. Readonly properties can only be set when an object is created and cannot be modified afterward. Here's an example:

```typescript
interface Point {

readonly x: number;

readonly y: number;

}

const point: Point = { x: 10, y: 20 };
```

console.log(point.x); *// Outputs: 10*

// Attempting to modify a readonly property will result in a compilation error

point.x = 15; *// Error: Cannot assign to 'x' because it is a read-only property.*

In this code, both x and y properties of the Point interface are marked as readonly, preventing any modifications after the object is created.

4. Function Signatures in Interfaces

Interfaces can also describe the shape of functions, including their parameter types and return types. This is useful when you want to enforce that objects implementing the interface must have a specific function with a particular signature. Here's an example:

```
interface Calculator {

add(x: number, y: number): number;

subtract(x: number, y: number): number;

}

const myCalculator: Calculator = {

add(x, y) {

return x + y;

},

subtract(x, y) {

return x - y;
```

```
},

};
```

In this code, the Calculator interface defines two function signatures: add and subtract. The myCalculator object implements these functions with the required parameter types and return types.

5. Type Aliases

Type aliases allow you to create custom names for types, which can simplify complex type definitions. They are particularly useful when you need to create reusable types or define union and intersection types. Here's an example:

```
type Point = {

x: number;

y: number;

};

const origin: Point = { x: 0, y: 0 };
```

In this code, we've created a type alias Point to define the structure of an object with x and y properties. Type aliases can be used in a manner similar to interfaces.

6. Union and Intersection Types

TypeScript allows you to create union and intersection types using the | and & operators, respectively. Union types represent values that can have one of several types, while intersection types combine multiple types into a single type. Here's an example:

```
type Student = {
```

```typescript
name: string;

studentId: number;

};

type Employee = {

name: string;

employeeId: string;

};

type Person = Student | Employee; // Union type

type StudentEmployee = Student & Employee; // Intersection type

const student: Person = {

name: "Alice",

studentId: 123,

};

const employee: StudentEmployee = {

name: "Bob",

studentId: 456,

employeeId: "emp123",

};
```

In this code, we've defined Student and Employee types and then created a Person type as a union of the two. Additionally, we've defined a StudentEmployee type as an intersection of Student and Employee.

7. Type Assertions

Type assertions are a way to tell TypeScript that you know more about the type of a value than it does. You can use the ` <

3.4 Classes and Inheritance

Classes are a fundamental concept in object-oriented programming, and TypeScript provides full support for defining and using classes. Classes enable you to create blueprints for objects, encapsulate data, and define methods to operate on that data. In this section, we'll explore how to define classes, work with constructors, and use inheritance in TypeScript.

1. Class Declaration

You can declare a class in TypeScript using the class keyword, followed by the class name. Here's a simple example of defining a Person class:

```
class Person {

firstName: string;

lastName: string;

constructor(firstName: string, lastName: string) {

this.firstName = firstName;

this.lastName = lastName;

}
```

```typescript
getFullName(): string {

return `${this.firstName} ${this.lastName}`;

}

}
```

In this code, we've defined a Person class with properties firstName and lastName. The class also has a constructor that accepts these properties as parameters and a getFullName method that returns the full name.

2. Creating Class Instances

To create an instance of a class, you use the new keyword followed by the class name and constructor arguments, if any. Here's how you create a Person instance:

```typescript
const alice = new Person("Alice", "Johnson");

console.log(alice.getFullName()); // Outputs: Alice Johnson
```

In this example, we've created a Person instance named alice with the specified first and last names and called the getFullName method to retrieve the full name.

3. Access Modifiers

TypeScript provides access modifiers like public, private, and protected to control the visibility and accessibility of class members. Here's a brief overview of these access modifiers:

- **Public**: Members marked as public are accessible from anywhere, both within and outside the class.

- **Private**: Members marked as private are only accessible within the class where they are defined. They cannot be accessed from outside the class.

- **Protected**: Members marked as protected are accessible within the class and its subclasses (derived classes).

Here's an example illustrating the use of access modifiers:

```
class BankAccount {

private balance: number;

constructor(initialBalance: number) {

this.balance = initialBalance;

}

deposit(amount: number): void {

this.balance += amount;

}

withdraw(amount: number): void {

if (amount <= this.balance) {

this.balance -= amount;

} else {

console.log("Insufficient funds.");

}

}
```

```typescript
}

class SavingsAccount extends BankAccount {

private interestRate: number;

constructor(initialBalance: number, interestRate: number) {

super(initialBalance);

this.interestRate = interestRate;

}

calculateInterest(): number {

return (this.balance * this.interestRate) / 100;

}

}

const savings = new SavingsAccount(1000, 2);

savings.deposit(500);

savings.withdraw(200);

console.log(savings.calculateInterest()); // Outputs: 14
```

In this code, the balance property of the BankAccount class is marked as private, making it inaccessible from outside the class. The SavingsAccount class extends BankAccount and has its own interestRate property. The calculateInterest method in SavingsAccount calculates the interest based on the balance and interest rate.

4. Inheritance

Inheritance is a key feature of object-oriented programming, and TypeScript supports it fully. You can create subclasses (derived classes) that inherit properties and methods from a superclass (base class). Here's an example:

```typescript
class Animal {

name: string;

constructor(name: string) {

this.name = name;

}

speak(): void {

console.log(`${this.name} makes a sound.`);

}

}

class Dog extends Animal {

constructor(name: string) {

super(name);

}

speak(): void {

console.log(`${this.name} barks.`);

}
```

```
}
```

const dog = **new** Dog("Buddy");

dog.speak(); // *Outputs: Buddy barks.*

In this code, we've defined an Animal class with a name property and a speak method. The Dog class extends Animal and overrides the speak method to provide its own implementation. When we create a Dog instance and call speak, it uses the overridden method.

5. Abstract Classes

Abstract classes are classes that cannot be instantiated directly but serve as blueprints for other classes. They may contain abstract methods that must be implemented by derived classes. Here's an example:

```
abstract class Shape {

abstract area(): number;

}

class Circle extends Shape {

radius: number;

constructor(radius: number) {

super();

this.radius = radius;

}

area(): number {
```

```typescript
return Math.PI * this.radius ** 2;

}

}

const circle = new Circle(5);

console.log(circle.area()); // Outputs: 78.53981633974483
```

In this code, the Shape class is marked as abstract and contains an abstract method area. The Circle class extends Shape and provides an implementation for the area method. Abstract classes can be used to define common behavior for subclasses while enforcing that specific methods are implemented.

6. Summary

Classes and inheritance are fundamental concepts in TypeScript that enable you to create structured and reusable code. You can define classes with properties and methods, use access modifiers to control visibility, and create subclasses that inherit and override functionality. Abstract classes provide a way to define common behavior and enforce method implementations in derived classes. Understanding these concepts is essential for building robust and organized TypeScript applications.

3.5 Modules and Namespaces

Modules and namespaces are TypeScript's way of organizing and encapsulating code to manage complexity and prevent naming conflicts in large applications. In this section, we'll explore how to use modules and namespaces in TypeScript to structure your code effectively.

1. Modules in TypeScript

A module in TypeScript is a self-contained unit of code that encapsulates related functionality, variables, classes, and interfaces. Modules allow you to keep your code organized and prevent polluting the global scope with variables and functions. Here's an example of defining a module and exporting its members:

// math.ts (module)

export const add = (a: number, b: number): number => a + b;

export const subtract = (a: number, b: number): number => a - b;

In this code, we've created a module named math.ts and exported two functions, add and subtract. To use these functions in another file, you can import them using the import statement:

// main.ts

import { add, subtract } **from** "./math";

console.log(add(5, 3)); *// Outputs: 8*

console.log(subtract(10, 4)); *// Outputs: 6*

By importing specific members from the math module, you can use them in your main.ts file without worrying about naming conflicts.

2. Default Exports

Modules can also have a default export, which is a single export that is treated as the module's "main" export. Here's an example:

// logger.ts (module)

const log = (message: string): void => {

```
console.log(message);

};
```

export default log;

In this code, the logger.ts module exports a single function, log, as the default export. You can import the default export without curly braces:

// main.ts

import log **from** "./logger";

log("Hello, TypeScript!"); *// Outputs: Hello, TypeScript!*

Default exports are particularly useful when a module has a primary functionality that you want to emphasize.

3. Re-exports

You can also re-export members from one module in another module. This can help with organizing your code and providing a single entry point for external consumers. Here's an example:

// utils.ts (module)

```
export const capitalize = (str: string): string => {

return str.charAt(0).toUpperCase() + str.slice(1);

};
```

// index.ts (module that re-exports)

export { capitalize } **from** "./utils";

In this code, the index.ts module re-exports the capitalize function from the utils.ts module. This allows consumers to import capitalize directly from the index.ts module.

4. Namespaces

Namespaces in TypeScript provide a way to organize related code in a single, named scope. Namespaces help prevent naming collisions and allow you to structure your code logically. Here's an example of defining and using a namespace:

```typescript
// shapes.ts (namespace)

namespace Shapes {

export class Circle {

constructor(public radius: number) {}

area(): number {

return Math.PI * this.radius ** 2;

}

}

}

// main.ts

const circle = new Shapes.Circle(5);

console.log(circle.area()); // Outputs: 78.53981633974483
```

In this code, we've defined a Shapes namespace that contains a Circle class. The main.ts file can access the Circle class within the Shapes namespace.

5. Ambient Declarations

Ambient declarations allow you to declare types and interfaces for external libraries or modules that don't have TypeScript type definitions. You can declare these types in a .d.ts file and use them in your TypeScript code. Here's an example:

```typescript
// my-library.d.ts (ambient declaration)

declare module "my-library" {

export function greet(name: string): string;

}

// main.ts

import { greet } from "my-library";

const message = greet("Alice");

console.log(message); // Outputs: Hello, Alice!
```

In this code, we've created an ambient declaration for the "my-library" module, specifying that it exports a greet function. This allows you to import and use greet in your TypeScript code as if it were a regular TypeScript module.

6. Summary

Modules and namespaces in TypeScript help you organize and structure your code effectively. You can use modules to encapsulate related functionality and prevent naming conflicts. Default exports provide a clear entry point for modules, and re-exports allow you to expose specific members from one module in another. Namespaces provide a way to create scoped containers for related code. Additionally, ambient declarations allow you to define types and interfaces for external libraries. Understanding how to use these features is crucial for building maintainable and scalable TypeScript applications.

Chapter 4: Advanced TypeScript Features

4.1 Generics in TypeScript

Generics in TypeScript provide a powerful way to write reusable and type-safe code. They allow you to create functions, classes, and interfaces that work with a variety of data types while maintaining type safety. Generics are commonly used in scenarios where you want to write code that can adapt to different data types without sacrificing type checking.

1. Introduction to Generics

Generics are often denoted by angle brackets (<>) and a type parameter, which is a placeholder for a specific data type. You can use this type parameter throughout your code to represent different types dynamically. Here's a basic example of a generic function:

```typescript
function identity<T>(arg: T): T {

return arg;

}

const result1 = identity("Hello, TypeScript"); // result1 is of type string

const result2 = identity(42); // result2 is of type number
```

In this code, the identity function is defined with a type parameter <T>. It takes an argument of type T and returns that argument. When calling identity, TypeScript infers the appropriate type based on the argument passed.

2. Using Generics with Arrays

Generics are commonly used with arrays to create reusable functions that work with arrays of different types. Here's an example of a generic function to reverse an array:

```typescript
function reverseArray<T>(arr: T[]): T[] {

return arr.reverse();

}

const numbers = [1, 2, 3, 4, 5];

const reversedNumbers = reverseArray(numbers); // reversedNumbers is of type number[]

const fruits = ["apple", "banana", "cherry"];

const reversedFruits = reverseArray(fruits); // reversedFruits is of type string[]
```

In this code, the reverseArray function uses a type parameter T to work with arrays of different types. It reverses the input array while preserving its type.

3. Generic Classes

You can also create generic classes in TypeScript. This allows you to define classes that can work with various data types. Here's an example of a generic stack class:

```typescript
class Stack<T> {

private items: T[] = [];

push(item: T): void {
```

```typescript
this.items.push(item);

}

pop(): T | undefined {

return this.items.pop();

}

isEmpty(): boolean {

return this.items.length === 0;

}

}

const numberStack = new Stack<number>();

numberStack.push(1);

numberStack.push(2);

numberStack.push(3);

const poppedNumber = numberStack.pop(); // poppedNumber is of
type number

const stringStack = new Stack<string>();

stringStack.push("apple");

stringStack.push("banana");

stringStack.push("cherry");

const poppedString = stringStack.pop(); // poppedString is of type
string
```

In this code, the Stack class is defined as a generic class with type parameter T. It can be instantiated with different data types, such as numbers and strings.

4. Constraints on Generics

You can add constraints to generics to restrict the types that can be used with them. This is useful when you want to ensure that certain properties or methods are available on the type parameter. Here's an example of a generic function with constraints:

```typescript
interface Printable {

print(): void;

}

function printIfPrintable<T extends Printable>(obj: T): void {

obj.print();

}

class Person implements Printable {

constructor(private name: string) {}

print(): void {

console.log(`Person's name: ${this.name}`);

}

}

const alice = new Person("Alice");

printIfPrintable(alice); // Calls the print method of the Person class
```

printIfPrintable("Hello"); *// Error: Argument of type 'string' is not assignable to parameter of type 'Printable'.*

In this code, the printIfPrintable function has a constraint <T extends Printable>, which means that the type parameter T must implement the Printable interface. It ensures that only objects with a print method can be passed to this function.

5. Summary

Generics are a powerful feature in TypeScript that allow you to write flexible and type-safe code. They are commonly used to create reusable functions, classes, and interfaces that work with a variety of data types. Generics can be constrained to ensure that specific properties or methods are available on the type parameter. Understanding how to use generics is essential for writing efficient and adaptable TypeScript code.

4.2 Decorators and Metadata

Decorators are a powerful feature in TypeScript that allow you to add metadata and behavior to classes, methods, properties, or parameters. They are often used in frameworks like Angular to enhance and extend the functionality of classes. In this section, we'll explore decorators in TypeScript and how they can be applied to various elements in your code.

1. Introduction to Decorators

Decorators are special functions that are prefixed with the @ symbol and can be applied to class declarations, method declarations, property declarations, or parameter declarations. They provide a way to add annotations and behavior to these elements. Here's a basic example of a class decorator:

```typescript
function MyDecorator(target: Function) {

// Add behavior to the class constructor

target.prototype.myProperty = "Hello, Decorator!";

}

@MyDecorator

class MyClass {}

const instance = new MyClass();

console.log(instance.myProperty); // Outputs: Hello, Decorator!
```

In this code, the @MyDecorator syntax applies the decorator to the MyClass class, and it adds a property to the class constructor.

2. Class Decorators

Class decorators are applied to class declarations and can be used to modify the class constructor or add metadata to the class. Here's an example of a class decorator that logs when a class is instantiated:

```typescript
function LogClass(target: Function) {

const original = target;

const newConstructor: any = function (...args: any[]) {

console.log(`Creating instance of ${original.name}`);

return new original(...args);

};

newConstructor.prototype = original.prototype;
```

```typescript
  return newConstructor;

}

@LogClass

class MyClass {}

const instance = new MyClass(); // Outputs: Creating instance of MyClass
```

In this code, the LogClass decorator intercepts the class instantiation process and logs a message before creating the instance.

3. Method Decorators

Method decorators are applied to methods within a class and can be used to modify the behavior of the method or add metadata. Here's an example of a method decorator that measures the execution time of a method:

```typescript
function MeasureTime(target: any, propertyKey: string, descriptor: PropertyDescriptor) {

const originalMethod = descriptor.value;

descriptor.value = function (...args: any[]) {

const start = Date.now();

const result = originalMethod.apply(this, args);

const end = Date.now();

console.log(`Method ${propertyKey} took ${end - start}ms to execute`);

return result;
```

```typescript
};

}

class MyClass {

@MeasureTime

slowOperation() {

// Simulate a slow operation

for (let i = 0; i < 100000000; i++) {}

}

}

const instance = new MyClass();

instance.slowOperation(); // Outputs: Method slowOperation took [time]ms to execute
```

In this code, the MeasureTime decorator measures the execution time of the slowOperation method and logs the duration.

4. Property Decorators

Property decorators are applied to class properties and can be used to add metadata or modify the property's behavior. Here's an example of a property decorator that ensures a property is always positive:

```typescript
function PositiveNumber(target: any, propertyKey: string) {

let value: number;

const getter = function () {

return value;
```

```typescript
};

const setter = function (newValue: number) {

if (newValue < 0) {

throw new Error(`Value of ${propertyKey} must be positive`);

}

value = newValue;

};

Object.defineProperty(target, propertyKey, {

get: getter,

set: setter,

enumerable: true,

configurable: true,

});

}

class MyCounter {

@PositiveNumber

count: number = 0;

}

const counter = new MyCounter();

counter.count = 5; // Valid
```

counter.count = -2; // *Throws an error: Value of count must be positive*

In this code, the PositiveNumber decorator ensures that the count property is always positive when assigned a value.

5. Parameter Decorators

Parameter decorators are applied to parameters of a method or constructor and can be used to add metadata or modify their behavior. Here's an example of a parameter decorator that logs the value of a method parameter:

```typescript
function LogParameter(target: any, propertyKey: string, parameterIndex: number) {

const originalMethod = target[propertyKey];

target[propertyKey] = function (...args: any[]) {

console.log(`Value of parameter at index ${parameterIndex}: ${args[parameterIndex]}`);

return originalMethod.apply(this, args);

};

}

class Calculator {

add(@LogParameter a: number, @LogParameter b: number): number {

return a + b;

}

}
```

```typescript
const calculator = new Calculator();

calculator.add(3, 5); // Outputs: Value of parameter at index 0: 3

// Value of parameter at index 1: 5
```

In this code, the LogParameter decorator logs the value of method parameters when the add method is called.

6. Decorator Factories

Decorator factories are functions that return decorator functions with parameters. This allows you to create more flexible and configurable decorators. Here's an example of a decorator factory that accepts a message:

```typescript
function LogWithMessage(message: string): MethodDecorator {

return function (target: any, propertyKey: string, descriptor: PropertyDescriptor) {

const originalMethod = descriptor.value;

descriptor.value = function (...args: any[]) {

console.log(`Message: ${message}`);

return originalMethod.apply(this, args);

};

};

}

class MyLogger {

@LogWithMessage("Starting calculation")
```

```typescript
calculate(a: number, b: number): number {

return a + b;

}

}

const logger = new MyLogger();

logger.calculate(3, 5); // Outputs: Message: Starting calculation
```

In this code, the LogWithMessage decorator factory accepts a message as a parameter and returns a method decorator that logs the message when the calculate method is called.

7. Summary

Decorators are a versatile feature in TypeScript that allow you to add metadata and behavior to various elements of your code, including classes, methods, properties, and parameters. They are commonly used in frameworks and libraries to extend and enhance the functionality of classes. Understanding how to use decorators is valuable for creating more flexible and expressive code in TypeScript.

4.3 Working with Enums

Enums (short for "enumerations") in TypeScript are a way to define a set of named constant values. They are a helpful tool for representing a fixed set of values, such as days of the week, status codes, or any other set of related constants. In this section, we'll explore how to work with enums in TypeScript.

1. Enum Basics

To define an enum in TypeScript, you use the enum keyword followed by a name for the enum and a list of named constants enclosed in curly braces. Here's a simple example of a Color enum:

```typescript
enum Color {

Red,

Green,

Blue,

}
```

In this code, we've defined a Color enum with three named constants: Red, Green, and Blue. By default, these constants are assigned numeric values starting from 0 for the first constant and incrementing by 1 for each subsequent constant. For example, Color.Red is equivalent to 0, Color.Green is equivalent to 1, and so on.

2. Using Enums

You can use enums to represent these constants in your code. Enums provide both a way to define the values and a way to access them. Here's how you can use the Color enum:

```typescript
let color: Color = Color.Green;

console.log(color); // Outputs: 1

if (color === Color.Green) {

console.log("The color is green.");
```

```
}
```

In this code, we've assigned the Color.Green constant to the color variable and then compared it to Color.Green in the if statement.

3. Custom Enum Values

While enums automatically assign numeric values, you can also specify custom values for enum constants. Here's an example:

```
enum ErrorCode {

NotFound = 404,

Unauthorized = 401,

InternalServerError = 500,

}
```

In this code, we've assigned custom numeric values to the ErrorCode enum constants. Now, ErrorCode.NotFound is 404, ErrorCode.Unauthorized is 401, and so on.

4. Reverse Mapping

Enums in TypeScript also support reverse mapping, which means you can convert a numeric value back to its corresponding enum constant. TypeScript generates this reverse mapping automatically for numeric enums. Here's an example:

```
enum Direction {

North,

East,

South,
```

West,

}

const direction = Direction.South;

console.log(Direction[direction]); // *Outputs: "South"*

In this code, we've defined a Direction enum and used reverse mapping to convert the numeric value 2 (which corresponds to Direction.South) back to the string "South".

5. Enums with String Values

While numeric enums are common, you can also create enums with string values. String enums don't have reverse mapping by default. Here's an example of a string enum:

enum Fruit {

Apple = "apple",

Banana = "banana",

Cherry = "cherry",

}

In this code, we've defined a Fruit enum with string values. Each enum constant is explicitly assigned a string value.

6. Heterogeneous Enums

In TypeScript, enums can also be heterogeneous, meaning they can have a mix of numeric and string values. Here's an example:

enum Status {

Active = 1,

Inactive = "inactive",

Pending = 2,

}

In this code, the Status enum has a mix of numeric and string values. This can be useful in certain scenarios, but it's important to use with care.

7. Summary

Enums in TypeScript are a valuable tool for defining sets of named constants. They help make your code more expressive and self-documenting by giving meaningful names to values. You can use enums to represent fixed sets of values and even customize the numeric or string values assigned to enum constants. Enums are widely used in TypeScript to improve code readability and maintainability. Understanding how to work with enums is essential for TypeScript developers.

4.4 Advanced Type Patterns

In TypeScript, advanced type patterns allow you to work with types in more flexible and sophisticated ways. These patterns involve combining and manipulating types to achieve specific goals, such as creating reusable utilities or modeling complex data structures. In this section, we'll explore some advanced type patterns and techniques in TypeScript.

1. Union Types

Union types allow you to represent a value that can be of one of several types. You define a union type by using the | operator between the types. Here's an example:

```
type Result = string | number;

const value1: Result = "Hello";

const value2: Result = 42;
```

In this code, the Result type can be either a string or a number. You can use union types to model scenarios where a variable can have multiple potential types.

2. Intersection Types

Intersection types allow you to combine multiple types into a single type. You define an intersection type by using the & operator between the types. Here's an example:

```
type Person = {

name: string;

};

type Address = {

city: string;

};

type ContactInfo = Person & Address;

const contact: ContactInfo = {
```

```
name: "Alice",

city: "New York",

};
```

In this code, the ContactInfo type is an intersection of Person and Address, allowing you to represent an object with properties from both types.

3. Conditional Types

Conditional types in TypeScript allow you to create types that depend on other types. They use conditional statements to determine the resulting type based on a condition. Here's an example:

```
type CheckType<T> = T extends string ? "string" : "non-string";

const result1: CheckType<string> = "string"; // "string"

const result2: CheckType<number> = "non-string"; // "non-string"
```

In this code, the CheckType type checks if the type T is a string and assigns either "string" or "non-string" as the resulting type.

4. Mapped Types

Mapped types in TypeScript allow you to create new types by transforming the properties of an existing type. You define mapped types using the keyof keyword and mapping functions. Here's an example:

```
type Person = {

name: string;
```

```typescript
age: number;

};

type ReadonlyPerson<T> = {

readonly [P in keyof T]: T[P];

};

const readonlyAlice: ReadonlyPerson<Person> = {

name: "Alice",

age: 30,

};
```

In this code, the ReadonlyPerson mapped type creates a new type with all properties of Person, but with the readonly modifier applied.

5. Recursive Types

Recursive types allow you to define types that reference themselves. This is useful for modeling recursive data structures, such as linked lists or tree structures. Here's a simplified example of a linked list type:

```typescript
type ListNode<T> = {

value: T;

next?: ListNode<T>;

};

const node1: ListNode<number> = { value: 1 };

const node2: ListNode<number> = { value: 2, next: node1 };
```

In this code, the ListNode type references itself through the next property, creating a linked list of values.

6. Conditional Index Signatures

Conditional index signatures allow you to define object types with dynamic property names based on a condition. Here's an example:

```typescript
type User = {

name: string;

};

type Admin = {

name: string;

role: "admin";

};

type UserType = "user" | "admin";

type UserInfo = {

[K in UserType]: K extends "admin" ? Admin : User;

};

const user: UserInfo = {

user: { name: "Alice" },

admin: { name: "Bob", role: "admin" },

};
```

In this code, the UserInfo type uses a conditional index signature to specify different property types based on the UserType.

7. Summary

Advanced type patterns in TypeScript allow you to work with types in more versatile ways. Union types, intersection types, conditional types, mapped types, recursive types, and conditional index signatures are powerful tools that enable you to model complex data structures and create flexible type systems. Understanding these advanced type patterns is essential for mastering TypeScript and building sophisticated applications with strong type checking.

4.5 Asynchronous Programming with Promises and Async/Await

Asynchronous programming is a fundamental aspect of modern web development, and TypeScript provides robust support for it. Promises and the async/await syntax are essential tools for managing asynchronous operations in TypeScript. In this section, we'll explore how to use Promises and async/await to work with asynchronous code effectively.

1. Promises

Promises are a way to handle asynchronous operations in a more organized and manageable manner. A Promise represents a value that may be available now, or in the future, or possibly never. Here's a basic example of creating and using a Promise in TypeScript:

```typescript
function fetchData(): Promise<string> {

return new Promise((resolve, reject) => {

setTimeout(() => {
```

```typescript
    resolve("Data fetched successfully!");
  }, 1000);

  });

}

fetchData()

  .then((result) => {

    console.log(result); // Outputs: "Data fetched successfully!"

  })

  .catch((error) => {

    console.error(error);

  });
```

In this code, the fetchData function returns a Promise that resolves with the data after a simulated delay. You can use .then() to handle the resolved value and .catch() to handle any errors that occur during the asynchronous operation.

2. Async/Await

The async/await syntax is a more concise and readable way to work with Promises in TypeScript. It allows you to write asynchronous code that resembles synchronous code. Here's how the previous example can be rewritten using async/await:

```typescript
async function fetchData(): Promise<string> {

  return new Promise((resolve) => {
```

```typescript
setTimeout(() => {

resolve("Data fetched successfully!");

}, 1000);

});

}

async function fetchDataAndLog() {

try {

const result = await fetchData();

console.log(result); // Outputs: "Data fetched successfully!"

} catch (error) {

console.error(error);

}

}

fetchDataAndLog();
```

In this code, the fetchData function is marked as async, and we use await to wait for the Promise to resolve. The fetchDataAndLog function also uses async/await to handle the asynchronous operation.

3. Promise Chaining

Promises can be chained together to execute asynchronous operations in a specific order. This is useful for performing multiple asynchronous tasks sequentially. Here's an example of Promise chaining:

```typescript
function fetchUserData(): Promise<{ id: number; username: string }> {

return new Promise((resolve) => {

setTimeout(() => {

resolve({ id: 1, username: "alice" });

}, 1000);

});

}

function fetchPosts(userId: number): Promise<string[]> {

return new Promise((resolve) => {

setTimeout(() => {

resolve([`Post 1 by User ${userId}`, `Post 2 by User ${userId}`]);

}, 1000);

});

}

fetchUserData()

.then((user) => fetchPosts(user.id))

.then((posts) => {

console.log(posts); // Outputs: ["Post 1 by User 1", "Post 2 by User 1"]
```

```
})

.catch((error) => {

console.error(error);

});
```

In this code, fetchUserData and fetchPosts functions return Promises, and we chain them together to fetch user data and then user posts sequentially.

4. Error Handling

Proper error handling is crucial in asynchronous code. Both Promises and async/await provide mechanisms for handling errors. In Promises, you can use .catch() to catch and handle errors. In async/await, you can use try/catch blocks to handle errors. Here's an example:

```
async function fetchUserData(): Promise<{ id: number; username: string }> {

return new Promise((resolve, reject) => {

setTimeout(() => {

// Simulate an error

reject("Error: Unable to fetch user data");

}, 1000);

});

}

async function fetchDataAndLog() {
```

```typescript
try {

const user = await fetchUserData();

console.log(user);

} catch (error) {

console.error(error); // Outputs: "Error: Unable to fetch user data"

}

}

fetchDataAndLog();
```

In this code, the fetchUserData function simulates an error, and we use try/catch to handle the error when calling fetchDataAndLog.

5. Summary

Promises and async/await are essential tools for working with asynchronous code in TypeScript. They make it easier to manage asynchronous operations, handle errors, and write more readable and maintainable code. Understanding how to use Promises and async/await is crucial for building responsive and efficient web applications in TypeScript.

Chapter 5: TypeScript and the DOM

5.1 Manipulating the DOM with TypeScript

Manipulating the Document Object Model (DOM) is a fundamental part of building web applications. The DOM represents the structured representation of a web page, and JavaScript or TypeScript is commonly used to interact with and modify it. In this section, we'll explore how to manipulate the DOM using TypeScript to create dynamic and interactive web applications.

1. Understanding the DOM

Before diving into DOM manipulation with TypeScript, it's crucial to understand the basic concepts of the DOM. The DOM is a hierarchical tree-like structure that represents the structure of an HTML document. Each element in an HTML document, such as <div>, <p>, or <a>, is a node in the DOM tree. You can access and manipulate these nodes using JavaScript or TypeScript.

2. Accessing DOM Elements

To access DOM elements in TypeScript, you can use the document object provided by the browser. Here's an example of how to select an element by its id attribute:

```typescript
const myElement = document.getElementById("my-element-id");

if (myElement) {

// Manipulate the element here

myElement.textContent = "Hello, DOM!";

}
```

In this code, we use getElementById to select an element with the specified id attribute. We then manipulate the element by changing its textContent.

3. Event Handling

Event handling is a crucial aspect of building interactive web applications. You can use TypeScript to attach event listeners to DOM elements and respond to user interactions. Here's an example of handling a click event:

```typescript
const button = document.getElementById("my-button-id");

if (button) {

button.addEventListener("click", () => {

alert("Button clicked!");

});

}
```

In this code, we select a button element by its id and attach a click event listener that displays an alert when the button is clicked.

4. Modifying DOM Elements

You can use TypeScript to modify the content and attributes of DOM elements dynamically. For example, you can change the text inside a paragraph element:

```typescript
const paragraph = document.getElementById("my-paragraph-id");

if (paragraph) {

paragraph.textContent = "Updated text content";
```

```
}
```

You can also modify element attributes, such as the src attribute of an image element or the href attribute of a link element.

5. Creating New DOM Elements

In addition to manipulating existing DOM elements, TypeScript allows you to create new elements and append them to the DOM. Here's an example of creating a new <div> element and appending it to the body:

```
const newDiv = document.createElement("div");

newDiv.textContent = "Newly created div";

document.body.appendChild(newDiv);
```

In this code, we use createElement to create a new <div> element, set its textContent, and then append it to the document.body.

6. Summary

Manipulating the DOM with TypeScript is a fundamental skill for web developers. It allows you to create dynamic and interactive web applications by selecting, modifying, and creating DOM elements. Understanding how to access elements, handle events, and make changes to the DOM is essential for building modern web applications with TypeScript.

5.2 Handling Events

Handling events is a crucial part of building interactive web applications. Events can be triggered by user actions, such as clicks, keypresses, or mouse movements. In this section, we'll explore how to handle events using TypeScript and the DOM.

1. Event Listeners

Event listeners are functions that respond to specific events on DOM elements. You can attach event listeners to elements to execute custom code when those events occur. Here's an example of attaching a click event listener to a button element:

```typescript
const button = document.getElementById("my-button-id");

if (button) {

button.addEventListener("click", () => {

// Code to execute when the button is clicked

alert("Button clicked!");

});

}
```

In this code, we select a button element by its id attribute and attach a click event listener using addEventListener. When the button is clicked, the code inside the listener function is executed.

2. Event Types

There are many types of events that can be handled in web applications. Some common event types include:

- click: Triggered when a mouse click occurs.

- keydown: Triggered when a key on the keyboard is pressed.

- keyup: Triggered when a key on the keyboard is released.

- mouseenter and mouseleave: Triggered when the mouse enters or leaves an element.

- submit: Triggered when a form is submitted.

You can attach event listeners to elements for any event type you want to handle.

3. Event Object

When an event occurs, an event object is passed to the event listener function. This event object contains information about the event, such as the type of event, the target element, and any additional data related to the event. Here's an example of accessing the event object:

```typescript
const button = document.getElementById("my-button-id");

if (button) {

button.addEventListener("click", (event) => {

// Accessing the event object

console.log(event.type); // Outputs: "click"

console.log(event.target); // Outputs: the button element that was clicked

});

}
```

In this code, the event parameter in the event listener function provides access to the event object.

4. Removing Event Listeners

You can also remove event listeners from elements when they are no longer needed. This is important to prevent memory leaks and avoid unwanted behavior. To remove an event listener, you need to reference the same function that was used to add the listener. Here's an example:

```
function clickHandler(event: Event) {

// Code to execute when the button is clicked

alert("Button clicked!");

}

const button = document.getElementById("my-button-id");

if (button) {

button.addEventListener("click", clickHandler);

// Later, you can remove the event listener

button.removeEventListener("click", clickHandler);

}
```

In this code, the clickHandler function is added as an event listener, and then it is later removed using removeEventListener.

5. Event Delegation

Event delegation is a technique where you attach a single event listener to a common ancestor of multiple elements instead of attaching individual listeners to each element. This is useful for handling events on dynamically created or large numbers of elements efficiently. Here's an example of event delegation:

```typescript
const list = document.getElementById("my-list-id");

if (list) {

list.addEventListener("click", (event) => {

if (event.target instanceof HTMLLIElement) {

// Code to execute when an <li> element is clicked

alert(`Clicked on list item: ${event.target.textContent}`);

}

});

}
```

In this code, we attach a click event listener to a ul element that contains multiple li elements. When an li element is clicked, the event bubbles up to the ul element, and the listener checks if the clicked target is an li element before executing the code.

6. Summary

Handling events in web applications is essential for creating interactive user experiences. TypeScript provides a straightforward way to attach event listeners to DOM elements, respond to user actions, and manipulate the DOM based on those events. Understanding event types, event objects, and event delegation is crucial for building responsive and user-friendly web applications with TypeScript and the DOM.

5.3 Working with Forms

Forms are a fundamental part of web applications, allowing users to input and submit data. In this section, we'll explore how to work with forms in TypeScript, including form elements, form validation, and form submission.

1. Form Elements

HTML forms consist of various form elements such as text fields, checkboxes, radio buttons, select boxes, and buttons. These elements can be accessed and manipulated using TypeScript. Here's an example of selecting a text input field by its id attribute and retrieving its value:

```typescript
const inputElement = document.getElementById("my-input-id") as HTMLInputElement;

if (inputElement) {

const inputValue = inputElement.value;

// Use the inputValue as needed

}
```

In this code, we cast the selected element to an HTMLInputElement to access its value property.

2. Form Submission

When a user submits a form, you can capture and handle the form submission using TypeScript. You can prevent the default form submission behavior and execute custom code instead. Here's an example of preventing form submission and logging form data:

```typescript
const formElement = document.getElementById("my-form-id") as
HTMLFormElement;

if (formElement) {

formElement.addEventListener("submit", (event) => {

event.preventDefault(); // Prevent the default form submission

const formData = new FormData(formElement);

for (const pair of formData.entries()) {

console.log(`${pair[0]}: ${pair[1]}`);

}

});

}
```

In this code, we prevent the default form submission behavior using event.preventDefault(). We then create a FormData object to access and log the form data.

3. Form Validation

Form validation ensures that user input meets specific criteria before submission. TypeScript can be used to validate form data by checking input values and displaying validation messages. Here's an example of validating a required text input field:

```typescript
const inputElement = document.getElementById("my-input-id") as
HTMLInputElement;

if (inputElement) {

const inputValue = inputElement.value.trim();
```

```typescript
if (inputValue === "") {

// Display a validation message

console.error("Input is required.");

} else {

// Valid input, proceed with form submission or other actions

console.log("Input is valid:", inputValue);

}

}
```

In this code, we check if the input value is empty (after trimming whitespace) and display a validation message if it is.

4. Dynamic Form Elements

You can dynamically add or remove form elements using TypeScript to create dynamic and interactive forms. For example, you can add input fields based on user interactions or requirements. Here's a simplified example of dynamically adding input fields:

```typescript
const addButton = document.getElementById("add-button-id");

const formElement = document.getElementById("my-form-id") as HTMLFormElement;

if (addButton && formElement) {

addButton.addEventListener("click", () => {

const newInput = document.createElement("input");

newInput.type = "text";
```

```
newInput.name = "dynamic-input"; // Set a unique name

formElement.appendChild(newInput);

});

}
```

In this code, we attach a click event listener to a button element that dynamically adds text input fields to a form when clicked.

5. Summary

Working with forms in TypeScript is essential for building web applications that collect and process user data. You can access and manipulate form elements, handle form submission, perform form validation, and create dynamic forms to provide a seamless user experience. Understanding how to work with forms in TypeScript is crucial for developing interactive and data-driven web applications.

5.4 DOM Manipulation Best Practices

When working with the Document Object Model (DOM) in web development with TypeScript, it's essential to follow best practices to ensure efficient, maintainable, and performant code. In this section, we'll discuss some best practices for DOM manipulation.

1. Minimize DOM Manipulation

Excessive DOM manipulation can lead to performance issues. Each time you modify the DOM, the browser must re-render the affected parts of the page, which can be costly in terms of CPU and memory usage. To optimize performance, minimize the number of DOM manipulations by grouping them together and using techniques like document fragments.

```javascript
// Inefficient

for (let i = 0; i < 100; i++) {

const newElement = document.createElement("div");

document.body.appendChild(newElement);

}

// More efficient

const fragment = document.createDocumentFragment();

for (let i = 0; i < 100; i++) {

const newElement = document.createElement("div");

fragment.appendChild(newElement);

}

document.body.appendChild(fragment);
```

In the inefficient example, we append elements one by one to the DOM, while the more efficient example uses a document fragment to minimize reflows.

2. Use Event Delegation

Event delegation is a technique where you attach a single event listener to a common ancestor of multiple elements instead of attaching individual listeners to each element. This is especially useful when dealing with a large number of similar elements or dynamically created elements.

```javascript
// Without event delegation
```

```typescript
const buttons = document.querySelectorAll(".my-button");

buttons.forEach((button) => {

button.addEventListener("click", () => {

// Handle button click

});

});

// With event delegation

const container = document.getElementById("button-container");

container.addEventListener("click", (event) => {

if (event.target.classList.contains("my-button")) {

// Handle button click

}

});
```

Event delegation reduces the number of event listeners and improves performance.

3. Cache DOM References

When working with the same DOM elements multiple times, it's a good practice to cache references to those elements to avoid unnecessary queries. This can improve code readability and performance.

```typescript
const myElement = document.getElementById("my-element-id");

const myButton = document.getElementById("my-button-id");
```

```
myButton.addEventListener("click", () => {
```

```
// Use myElement without querying the DOM again
```

```
myElement.textContent = "Button clicked!";
```

```
});
```

In this example, we cache references to myElement and myButton, ensuring that we don't need to query the DOM repeatedly.

4. Use Modern DOM APIs

Modern browsers provide efficient DOM manipulation APIs and methods that are faster and more convenient than older approaches. Whenever possible, use these modern APIs like querySelector, classList, and textContent.

```
const myElement = document.querySelector("#my-element-id");
```

```
myElement.classList.add("highlight");
```

```
myElement.textContent = "Updated content";
```

These modern APIs are more readable and maintainable than older methods like getElementById and direct property manipulation.

5. Avoid Inline JavaScript

Avoid using inline JavaScript attributes like onclick in your HTML markup. Instead, attach event listeners programmatically using TypeScript or JavaScript. This separation of concerns makes your code more organized and easier to maintain.

```
<!--Avoid-->
```

```
<button onclick="handleClick()">Click me</button>
```

```
<!--Preferred-->

<button id="my-button">Click me</button>

const button = document.getElementById("my-button");

button.addEventListener("click", () => {

// Handle button click

});
```

6. Use a Framework or Library

Consider using a JavaScript framework or library like React, Angular, or Vue.js if you're building complex web applications. These frameworks provide abstractions for DOM manipulation, state management, and more, which can lead to more organized and maintainable code.

By following these best practices, you can ensure that your DOM manipulation code in TypeScript is efficient, readable, and robust, leading to a better user experience in your web applications.

5.5 Building a Simple Web Application

In this section, we'll walk through the process of building a simple web application using TypeScript and DOM manipulation. We'll create a basic to-do list application to demonstrate how to interact with the DOM to add, delete, and update tasks.

1. HTML Structure

Let's start by defining the HTML structure for our to-do list. We'll have an input field for adding tasks, a list to display tasks, and buttons for adding and deleting tasks.

```html
<!DOCTYPE html>
<html lang="en">
<head>
<meta charset="UTF-8">
<meta name="viewport" content="width=device-width, initial-scale=1.0">
<title>Simple To-Do List</title>
</head>
<body>
<h1>Simple To-Do List</h1>
<input type="text" id="task-input" placeholder="Add a new task">
<button id="add-button">Add</button>
<ul id="task-list"></ul>
<button id="clear-button">Clear Completed</button>
</body>
</html>
```

2. TypeScript Code

Next, we'll write TypeScript code to handle interactions with the DOM. We'll select elements by their IDs and attach event listeners.

```
// Select DOM elements
```

```typescript
const taskInput = document.getElementById("task-input") as HTMLInputElement;

const addButton = document.getElementById("add-button");

const taskList = document.getElementById("task-list") as HTMLUListElement;

const clearButton = document.getElementById("clear-button");

// Event listener for adding tasks

addButton.addEventListener("click", () => {

const taskText = taskInput.value.trim();

if (taskText !== "") {

// Create a new list item

const listItem = document.createElement("li");

listItem.textContent = taskText;

// Add a delete button

const deleteButton = document.createElement("button");

deleteButton.textContent = "Delete";

deleteButton.addEventListener("click", () => {

taskList.removeChild(listItem);

});

listItem.appendChild(deleteButton);

taskList.appendChild(listItem);
```

```javascript
// Clear the input field

taskInput.value = "";

}

});

// Event listener for clearing completed tasks

clearButton.addEventListener("click", () => {

const completedTasks = taskList.querySelectorAll("li");

completedTasks.forEach((task) => {

if (task.querySelector("button")) {

taskList.removeChild(task);

}

});

});
```

3. Styling with CSS

We can enhance the visual appearance of our to-do list using CSS. Here's a basic example:

```css
body {

font-family: Arial, sans-serif;

text-align: center;

margin: 0;
```

```css
padding: 0;

background-color: #f0f0f0;

}

h1 {

color: #333;

}

#task-input {

padding: 10px;

width: 60%;

border: 1px solid #ccc;

}

button {

padding: 10px 20px;

margin: 10px;

background-color: #007bff;

color: white;

border: none;

cursor: pointer;

}

ul {
```

```css
list-style: none;

padding: 0;

}

li {

background-color: white;

padding: 10px;

margin: 10px;

border: 1px solid #ccc;

display: flex;

justify-content: space-between;

align-items: center;

}

button {

background-color: #d9534f;

}
```

This CSS provides a simple and clean style for our to-do list.

4. Conclusion

By following these steps, we've created a basic web application for managing tasks. Users can add new tasks, mark them as completed, and clear completed tasks. This example demonstrates how TypeScript and DOM manipulation can be used to create interactive web applications. You can further enhance and customize this application to suit your needs and explore more advanced features and functionality.

Chapter 6: Building Modular Applications

6.1 Organizing Your Codebase

Organizing your codebase is a crucial aspect of building maintainable and scalable applications in TypeScript. A well-structured codebase makes it easier to collaborate with other developers and maintain the project over time. In this section, we'll explore various techniques and best practices for organizing your TypeScript codebase.

1. Project Structure

One of the first steps in organizing your TypeScript codebase is defining a clear project structure. A common approach is to use a folder structure that separates different parts of your application. Here's a simplified example of a project structure:

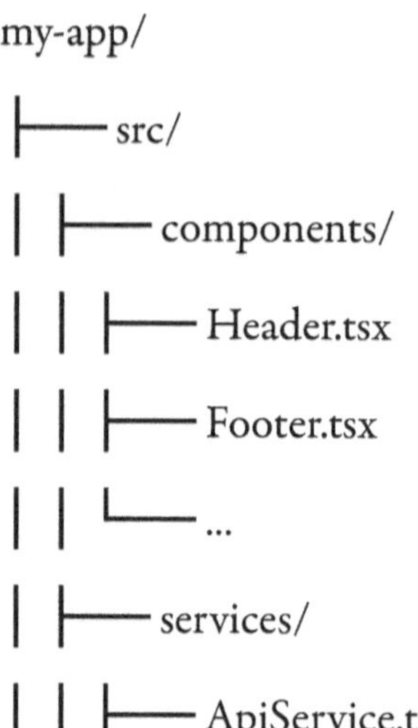

```
│   │   ├── AuthService.ts
│   │   └── ...
│   ├── utils/
│   │   ├── helpers.ts
│   │   ├── constants.ts
│   │   └── ...
│   ├── pages/
│   │   ├── Home.tsx
│   │   ├── About.tsx
│   │   └── ...
│   ├── index.tsx
│   └── ...
├── public/
│   ├── index.html
│   ├── images/
│   ├── styles/
│   └── ...
├── tsconfig.json
├── package.json
└── ...
```

In this example, we have organized our code into folders like components, services, utils, and pages. This separation helps maintain a clean and logical structure for different parts of the application.

2. Modularization

Modularization is a key concept in TypeScript development. You can break your code into smaller modules that encapsulate specific functionality. TypeScript supports both CommonJS and ES6 module systems, allowing you to use import and export statements to define dependencies between modules.

For example, in a file named utils/helpers.ts, you can export utility functions like this:

```
// utils/helpers.ts

export function calculateSum(a: number, b: number): number {

return a + b;

}

export function generateRandomNumber(): number {

return Math.random();

}
```

You can then import these functions in other parts of your codebase:

```
// src/components/Calculator.tsx

import { calculateSum } from '../utils/helpers';

function addNumbers(a: number, b: number): number {
```

return calculateSum(a, b);

}

This modular approach improves code reusability and maintainability.

3. TypeScript Configuration

To ensure consistency and type safety across your codebase, configure TypeScript using a tsconfig.json file. This file defines compiler options and settings for your TypeScript project. It can include settings for module resolution, target ECMAScript version, and more.

Here's a minimal tsconfig.json example:

{

"compilerOptions": {

"target": "ES2021",

"module": "CommonJS",

"strict": **true**,

"jsx": "react",

"outDir": "./dist"

},

"include": ["src/**/*.ts", "src/**/*.tsx"],

"exclude": ["node_modules"]

}

This configuration file specifies that TypeScript should target ECMAScript 2021, use the CommonJS module system, enforce strict type checking, and compile JSX to React code. The include and exclude options define which files should be included in the compilation process.

4. Code Linting and Formatting

Integrating a code linter and formatter like ESLint and Prettier into your TypeScript project can help maintain code quality and consistency. You can configure these tools to enforce coding standards and automatically format your code.

```
my-app/

├── .eslintrc.js

├── .prettierrc.js

└── ...
```

These configuration files allow you to define rules and formatting preferences for your project.

5. Dependency Management

Use a package manager like npm or yarn to manage external dependencies in your TypeScript project. You can define project dependencies in the package.json file and install them using the package manager.

```
{

"dependencies": {

"react": "^17.0.2",
```

```
"react-dom": "^17.0.2",

"axios": "^0.21.1"

},

"devDependencies": {

"@types/react": "^17.0.38",

"typescript": "^4.5.4",

"eslint": "^7.24.0",

"prettier": "^2.3.0"

}

}
```

Using a package manager simplifies the process of adding, updating, and managing dependencies.

6. Version Control

Utilize version control systems like Git to track changes in your codebase. Git allows you to collaborate with other developers, maintain a history of code changes, and revert to previous versions if needed.

7. Documentation

Documenting your code is essential for making it understandable to others (including your future self). Use comments, documentation tools like JSDoc, and README files to explain how different parts of your code work.

By following these best practices for organizing your TypeScript codebase, you can create a maintainable and scalable application structure that fosters collaboration and long-term development.

Remember that the specific organization and practices may vary depending on your project's size and complexity, but these principles provide a solid foundation for effective TypeScript development.

6.2 Dependency Injection in TypeScript

Dependency injection is a design pattern commonly used in TypeScript and other object-oriented programming languages. It's a technique that helps manage the dependencies between different components or services in your application. In this section, we'll explore the concept of dependency injection in TypeScript and how it can benefit your project.

1. What is Dependency Injection?

Dependency injection is a way to provide dependencies (usually other objects or services) to a class or function instead of creating them within the class or function itself. This decouples the code and makes it more modular and testable. Dependencies can be injected through constructor parameters, method parameters, or property setters.

Here's a basic example of dependency injection using constructor parameters in TypeScript:

```typescript
class UserService {

constructor(private userRepository: UserRepository) {}
getUserById(id: number) {
```

```typescript
    return this.userRepository.findById(id);

  }

}

class UserRepository {

  findById(id: number) {

    // Database query logic here

    return { id, name: 'John' };

  }

}

const userRepository = new UserRepository();

const userService = new UserService(userRepository);

const user = userService.getUserById(1);

console.log(user); // { id: 1, name: 'John' }
```

In this example, the UserService class depends on the UserRepository class. Instead of creating an instance of UserRepository inside UserService, we pass it as a constructor parameter, allowing us to easily swap it with a different implementation for testing or other purposes.

2. Benefits of Dependency Injection

Dependency injection offers several advantages in TypeScript and software development in general:

- **Testability:** It makes it easier to write unit tests for individual components because you can inject mock or stub dependencies during testing.

- **Flexibility:** You can swap implementations of dependencies without modifying the code that depends on them. This is useful for achieving different behaviors in different environments (e.g., development, production, testing).

- **Decoupling:** It reduces tight coupling between components, making the codebase more maintainable and adaptable to changes.

- **Readability:** Code that uses dependency injection is often more readable and self-explanatory because it clearly states its dependencies.

3. Dependency Injection Containers

In larger applications, managing dependencies manually can become complex. Dependency injection containers (also known as DI containers or IoC containers) are tools that help automate the process of resolving and injecting dependencies. Popular DI containers for TypeScript and JavaScript include InversifyJS and NestJS's built-in DI system.

Here's a simplified example of how InversifyJS can be used:

```typescript
import { Container, injectable, inject } from 'inversify';

@injectable()
class UserService {
```

```typescript
constructor(@inject('UserRepository') private userRepository:
UserRepository) {}

getUserById(id: number) {

return this.userRepository.findById(id);

}

}

@injectable()

class UserRepository {

findById(id: number) {

// Database query logic here

return { id, name: 'John' };

}

}

const container = new Container();

container.bind<UserRepository>('UserRepository').to(UserRepository);

container.bind<UserService>('UserService').to(UserService);

const userService = container.get<UserService>('UserService');

const user = userService.getUserById(1);

console.log(user); // { id: 1, name: 'John' }
```

In this example, we use InversifyJS to define and manage the dependencies between UserService and UserRepository. The container resolves and injects the dependencies automatically.

4. Conclusion

Dependency injection is a powerful technique for managing dependencies in TypeScript applications. It promotes modularity, testability, and maintainability by decoupling components and making them more flexible. Consider incorporating dependency injection into your TypeScript projects, especially as they grow in complexity, to reap the benefits it offers in terms of code quality and maintainability.

6.3 Building Reusable Components

Building reusable components is a fundamental concept in modern web development. In this section, we'll explore how to create reusable components in TypeScript, which is particularly relevant when working with frameworks like React, Angular, or Vue.js.

1. What Are Reusable Components?

Reusable components are self-contained units of code that encapsulate a specific piece of functionality or user interface (UI). They can be used multiple times throughout an application, promoting code reusability and maintainability. Reusable components are a core concept in component-based development frameworks like React and Angular.

2. Creating Reusable Components in TypeScript

When creating reusable components in TypeScript, there are some key principles to keep in mind:

2.1. Component Composition

Components should be designed to be composed together to create complex UIs. For example, you can create a Button component and a TextInput component, and then compose them to build a LoginForm component.

```tsx
// Button.tsx

import React from 'react';

interface ButtonProps {

label: string;

onClick: () => void;

}

const Button: React.FC<ButtonProps> = ({ label, onClick }) => {

return <button onClick={onClick}>{label}</button>;

};

export default Button;

// TextInput.tsx

import React from 'react';

interface TextInputProps {

value: string;

onChange: (value: string) => void;

}
```

```tsx
const TextInput: React.FC<TextInputProps> = ({ value, onChange
}) => {

return <input type="text" value={value} onChange={(e) =>
onChange(e.target.value)} />;

};

export default TextInput;

// LoginForm.tsx

import React, { useState } from 'react';

import Button from './Button';

import TextInput from './TextInput';

const LoginForm: React.FC = () => {

const [username, setUsername] = useState("");

const [password, setPassword] = useState("");

const handleLogin = () => {

// Perform login logic

};

return (

<div>

<TextInput value={username} onChange={setUsername} />

<TextInput value={password} onChange={setPassword}
type="password" />
```

```
<Button label="Login" onClick={handleLogin} />

</div>

);

};
```

export default LoginForm;

2.2. Props and Composition

Passing props (properties) to components is a common way to customize their behavior and appearance. In the example above, we pass props like label, onClick, value, and onChange to customize the Button and TextInput components.

2.3. Reusability and Encapsulation

Design components to be highly reusable and encapsulated. They should be self-contained and not rely on global state or external dependencies whenever possible.

3. TypeScript and Type Safety

TypeScript provides strong type checking for your components, helping catch errors at compile time. When defining component props and state, use TypeScript's type annotations to ensure type safety.

4. Third-Party Libraries

Consider using third-party component libraries to save development time and benefit from well-tested, reusable components. Popular libraries like Material-UI, Ant Design, and Bootstrap offer a wide range of pre-built components that can be easily integrated into your TypeScript projects.

5. Documentation and Examples

When building reusable components, it's essential to provide clear documentation and usage examples for other developers who might use your components. Tools like Storybook can help create component documentation and showcase examples.

6. Testing

Write tests for your reusable components to ensure they behave correctly in various scenarios. Testing frameworks like Jest and tools like React Testing Library are commonly used for testing React components.

7. Conclusion

Creating reusable components is a crucial skill in TypeScript web development. By designing components with composition, props, and type safety in mind, you can build maintainable and scalable applications. Reusable components not only improve code organization but also enhance collaboration among developers and accelerate the development process.

6.4 Testing and Debugging Modules

Testing and debugging are integral parts of building modular applications in TypeScript. In this section, we'll explore the importance of testing and debugging modules, along with best practices and tools to streamline these processes.

1. Importance of Testing

Testing is critical to ensure the correctness and reliability of your modules. Modules can be unit-tested, integration-tested, or end-to-end tested, depending on their complexity and dependencies. Here are some key aspects of testing modules:

- **Unit Testing:** Focuses on testing individual functions or components in isolation. Use tools like Jest, Mocha, or Jasmine for unit testing in TypeScript.

- **Integration Testing:** Tests how different modules or components work together. It verifies that the interactions between modules produce the expected results.

- **End-to-End Testing:** Validates the entire application's functionality, often using tools like Cypress or Selenium. This type of testing simulates real user interactions.

2. Writing Tests

When writing tests for your modules, follow these best practices:

- Write descriptive test case names that explain what the test does.

- Isolate tests by providing mock data or dependencies when needed.

- Use assertion libraries like Chai or built-in assertion methods to check expected outcomes.

- Ensure that tests are reliable and repeatable, with no external dependencies or side effects.

- Automate your tests and run them as part of your development workflow.

// Example unit test using Jest

```typescript
import { add, subtract } from './math';

test('add function should return the sum of two numbers', () => {

const result = add(5, 3);

expect(result).toBe(8);

});

test('subtract function should return the difference between two numbers', () => {

const result = subtract(10, 4);

expect(result).toBe(6);

});
```

3. Debugging Modules

Debugging is the process of identifying and fixing issues or bugs in your modules. TypeScript provides excellent debugging support when combined with IDEs like Visual Studio Code. Here are some debugging tips:

- Use breakpoints to pause execution and inspect variable values.

- Utilize the debugging console for logging and interacting with your code during debugging.

- Step through code execution to understand its flow and identify issues.

- Take advantage of TypeScript's type checking to catch type-related errors during development.

4. Debugging Tools

Several tools and techniques can aid in debugging TypeScript modules:

- **Debugger Statements:** Insert debugger; statements in your code to trigger breakpoints when executed in a debugging environment.

- **Console Logging:** Use console.log() to output variable values and debug information.

- **Browser DevTools:** When working with TypeScript for the web, browser DevTools offer powerful debugging capabilities.

- **TypeScript Source Maps:** Ensure that your TypeScript compiler generates source maps (sourceMap configuration) to map generated JavaScript back to TypeScript source code.

5. Continuous Integration (CI) and Continuous Deployment (CD)

Integrate testing into your CI/CD pipeline to automatically run tests and catch errors early in the development process. Tools like Jenkins, Travis CI, or GitHub Actions can automate testing and deployment tasks.

6. Debugging Production Issues

To debug issues in production, consider using remote debugging tools and logging solutions. Tools like Sentry, LogRocket, or custom error reporting can help identify and resolve issues reported by users.

7. Conclusion

Testing and debugging are crucial aspects of building modular applications in TypeScript. By following best practices, writing comprehensive tests, and using effective debugging techniques and tools, you can ensure the reliability and maintainability of your modules. Incorporating testing and debugging into your development workflow will save time and effort in the long run and lead to more robust and error-free applications.

6.5 Packaging and Bundling with TypeScript

Packaging and bundling are essential steps in preparing TypeScript modules and applications for deployment. These processes involve organizing and optimizing your code, assets, and dependencies to improve load times and reduce the number of HTTP requests. In this section, we'll explore packaging and bundling techniques in TypeScript.

1. Why Packaging and Bundling?

1.1. Reducing HTTP Requests

Browsers have a limit on the number of parallel HTTP requests they can make to fetch resources. By bundling multiple files into a single bundle, you reduce the number of requests, which can significantly improve page load times.

1.2. Minimizing Network Latency

Smaller file sizes lead to faster downloads, particularly for users with slower internet connections or in regions with higher latency. Bundling and minifying your code and assets can reduce the overall file size.

1.3. Code Organization

Bundling allows you to organize your codebase better. Instead of referencing individual script files, you work with a single bundled file, making it easier to manage and maintain.

2. Tools for Packaging and Bundling

2.1. Webpack

Webpack is a widely used bundler for TypeScript applications. It can bundle TypeScript, JavaScript, CSS, and other assets. With plugins like ts-loader and babel-loader, you can seamlessly integrate TypeScript into your Webpack configuration.

2.2. Rollup

Rollup is another bundler commonly used for creating libraries and packages. It's known for its tree-shaking capabilities, which remove unused code during the bundling process, resulting in smaller bundle sizes.

2.3. Parcel

Parcel is a zero-config bundler that simplifies the bundling process. It automatically detects and bundles assets, making it a great choice for quick project setups.

3. Setting Up Bundling with TypeScript

Here's a simplified example of bundling TypeScript code with Webpack:

```javascript
// webpack.config.js

const path = require('path');

module.exports = {

entry: './src/index.ts', // Entry point

output: {

filename: 'bundle.js', // Output file name

path: path.resolve(__dirname, 'dist'), // Output directory

},

module: {

rules: [

{

test: /\.tsx?$/, // Match TypeScript files

use: 'ts-loader', // Use ts-loader for TypeScript files

exclude: /node_modules/, // Exclude node_modules
```

```
  },

  ],

},

resolve: {

  extensions: ['.tsx', '.ts', '.js'], // File extensions to resolve

},

};
```

In this example, we configure Webpack to bundle a TypeScript entry file (index.ts) into a single JavaScript bundle (bundle.js) in the dist directory.

4. Minification and Optimization

After bundling, it's common to minify and optimize the generated JavaScript and CSS files. Minification removes unnecessary whitespace and renames variables to reduce file sizes. Popular minification tools include Terser for JavaScript and CSSNano for CSS.

5. Code Splitting

Code splitting is a technique that allows you to split your code into multiple bundles, which can be loaded on demand. This is especially useful for large applications, as it reduces the initial load time.

6. CDN Deployment

Content Delivery Networks (CDNs) can help distribute your bundled assets globally, reducing server load and improving delivery speeds for users around the world.

7. Conclusion

Packaging and bundling are crucial steps in optimizing your TypeScript applications for production. By reducing HTTP requests, minimizing network latency, and improving code organization, you can provide a better user experience and faster load times. Choose the bundling tool that best fits your project's needs and incorporate it into your build process to streamline the deployment of your TypeScript applications.

Chapter 7: Managing State with TypeScript

7.1 State Management in Web Applications

State management is a critical aspect of building web applications, especially as they grow in complexity. Managing the state of your application involves handling and storing data that can change over time, such as user input, server responses, and UI interactions. In this section, we'll explore the importance of state management and various approaches to handle it in TypeScript applications.

1. The Importance of State Management

1.1. User Interactions

Web applications are interactive by nature, and user interactions can trigger changes in the application's state. For example, clicking a button, filling out a form, or toggling a switch can all result in state changes.

1.2. Server Data

Web applications often need to fetch data from servers or APIs. The retrieved data becomes part of the application's state and needs to be managed and displayed appropriately.

1.3. Component Communication

In component-based frameworks like React, Angular, and Vue.js, components may need to communicate and share state with each other. Effective state management ensures consistent data flow between components.

2. Local Component State

2.1. Component-Level State

For simpler applications or components, managing state at the component level is sufficient. Component-level state is maintained within a single component and can be accessed and updated locally. React's useState hook is an example of local state management.

```
import React, { useState } from 'react';

function Counter() {

const [count, setCount] = useState(0);

const increment = () => {

setCount(count + 1);

};

return (

<div>

<p>Count: {count}</p>

<button onClick={increment}>Increment</button>

</div>

);

}
```

2.2. Pros and Cons

- **Pros:** Simple and suitable for managing isolated state. Easy to set up and use.

- **Cons:** Not suitable for sharing state between components, especially when components are deeply nested or unrelated.

3. Global State Management

3.1. Context API (React)

React's Context API allows you to create global state accessible to all components in the component tree. It's a convenient way to share state without having to pass props down multiple levels of components.

```typescript
import React, { createContext, useContext, useState } from 'react';

const MyContext = createContext();

function MyProvider({ children }) {

const [data, setData] = useState({ /* initial data */ });

return (

<MyContext.Provider value={{ data, setData }}>

{children}

</MyContext.Provider>

);
```

```
}

function ComponentUsingContext() {

const { data, setData } = useContext(MyContext);

// Use data and setData

}
```

3.2. Pros and Cons

- **Pros:** Allows for global state sharing without prop drilling. Works well for medium-sized applications.

- **Cons:** Can become complex for large applications with many shared states. Requires additional libraries for advanced features like state persistence and asynchronous actions.

4. State Management Libraries

For larger and more complex applications, state management libraries like Redux, Mobx, and Zustand provide powerful tools for managing global state. These libraries offer features like predictable state changes, time-travel debugging, and optimized re-renders.

```
// Redux Example

import { configureStore, createSlice } from '@reduxjs/toolkit';

const counterSlice = createSlice({

name: 'counter',

initialState: 0,
```

```typescript
reducers: {

increment: (state) => state + 1,

decrement: (state) => state - 1,

},

});

const store = configureStore({

reducer: {

counter: counterSlice.reducer,

},

});

// Usage in React component

import { useSelector, useDispatch } from 'react-redux';

function Counter() {

const count = useSelector((state) => state.counter);

const dispatch = useDispatch();

const increment = () => {

dispatch(counterSlice.actions.increment());

};

}
```

5. Conclusion

State management is a fundamental aspect of web application development. Depending on the complexity of your application, you can choose between local component state, context API, or state management libraries to effectively manage and share state across components. The choice of state management approach should align with the specific needs and size of your application.

7.2 Using Redux with TypeScript

Redux is a popular state management library for building JavaScript and TypeScript applications, especially in the context of React applications. It provides a predictable state container that can be used in any JavaScript or TypeScript application, making it a powerful tool for managing application-wide state. In this section, we will explore how to use Redux with TypeScript.

1. Setting Up Redux with TypeScript

To use Redux with TypeScript, you'll need to install the necessary packages:

npm install redux @reduxjs/toolkit react-redux @types/react-redux

- redux is the core Redux library.

- @reduxjs/toolkit provides utilities for working with Redux and simplifies many common tasks.

- react-redux allows you to integrate Redux with React.

- @types/react-redux provides TypeScript type definitions for react-redux.

2. Creating a Redux Store

In Redux, the central piece is the store, which holds the application state. You define a store by creating a Redux slice using createSlice from @reduxjs/toolkit:

// counterSlice.ts

```ts
import { createSlice } from '@reduxjs/toolkit';

interface CounterState {

value: number;

}

const initialState: CounterState = {

value: 0,

};

const counterSlice = createSlice({

name: 'counter',

initialState,

reducers: {

increment: (state) => {

state.value += 1;

},

decrement: (state) => {

state.value -= 1;
```

```
  },

  },

});
```

export const { increment, decrement } = counterSlice.actions;

export default counterSlice.reducer;

3. Configuring the Redux Store

You configure the Redux store using configureStore from @reduxjs/toolkit:

// store.ts

import { configureStore } **from** '@reduxjs/toolkit';

import counterReducer **from** './counterSlice';

const store = configureStore({

reducer: {

counter: counterReducer,

},

});

export default store;

4. Using Redux in a React Component

To use Redux in a React component, you can use the useSelector and useDispatch hooks provided by react-redux:

import React **from** 'react';

```tsx
import { useSelector, useDispatch } from 'react-redux';

import { increment, decrement } from './counterSlice';

function Counter() {

const count = useSelector((state) => state.counter.value);

const dispatch = useDispatch();

return (

<div>

<p>Count: {count}</p>

<button onClick={() => dispatch(increment())}>Increment</button>

<button onClick={() => dispatch(decrement())}>Decrement</button>

</div>

);

}

export default Counter;
```

5. Strong Typing with Redux and TypeScript

One of the advantages of using TypeScript with Redux is the strong typing it provides. TypeScript can infer and enforce types for your Redux store, actions, and selectors, leading to fewer runtime errors.

6. Middleware and Advanced Configuration

Redux also supports middleware, which can be used for tasks like asynchronous actions (e.g., making API requests). Popular middleware for TypeScript applications includes redux-thunk and redux-saga.

7. Conclusion

Using Redux with TypeScript is a powerful combination for managing state in your React or TypeScript applications. It provides a predictable and type-safe way to manage complex application states. By defining actions, reducers, and selectors with TypeScript type annotations, you can catch many potential errors during development and build robust and maintainable applications.

7.3 Implementing State in Angular

Angular is another popular frontend framework that benefits from strong state management. In this section, we'll explore how to implement state management in Angular applications using various techniques and libraries, including Angular services and NgRx.

1. Angular Services for State Management

Angular provides a built-in way to manage application state using services. You can create a service to hold and manipulate your application's state and inject it into components that need access to the state.

1.1. Creating a State Service

// counter.service.ts

```typescript
import { Injectable } from '@angular/core';

@Injectable({

providedIn: 'root',

})

export class CounterService {

private count = 0;

increment() {

this.count++;

}

decrement() {

this.count—;

}

getCount() {

return this.count;

}

}
```

1.2. Using the State Service in a Component

```typescript
// counter.component.ts

import { Component } from '@angular/core';

import { CounterService } from './counter.service';
```

```typescript
@Component({
selector: 'app-counter',
template: `
<p>Count: {{ count }}</p>
<button (click)="increment()">Increment</button>
<button (click)="decrement()">Decrement</button>
`,
})
export class CounterComponent {
constructor(private counterService: CounterService) {}
get count() {
return this.counterService.getCount();
}
increment() {
this.counterService.increment();
}
decrement() {
this.counterService.decrement();
}
}
```

2. NgRx for Advanced State Management

For more complex state management scenarios in Angular applications, you can use NgRx, a popular state management library inspired by Redux.

2.1. Setting Up NgRx

To get started with NgRx, you'll need to install the required packages:

npm install @ngrx/store @ngrx/effects @ngrx/entity @ngrx/store-devtools

2.2. Creating Actions, Reducers, and Effects

NgRx uses actions, reducers, and effects to manage state:

- **Actions**: Actions are plain objects that represent an intention to change the state.

- **Reducers**: Reducers specify how the state changes in response to actions.

- **Effects**: Effects allow you to handle side effects like making HTTP requests.

// counter.actions.ts

```typescript
import { createAction } from '@ngrx/store';

export const increment = createAction('[Counter Component] Increment');
```

```typescript
export const decrement = createAction('[Counter Component] Decrement');
```

```typescript
// counter.reducer.ts

import { createReducer, on } from '@ngrx/store';

import { increment, decrement } from './counter.actions';

export const initialState = 0;

export const counterReducer = createReducer(

initialState,

on(increment, (state) => state + 1),

on(decrement, (state) => state - 1)

);
```

2.3. Setting Up the Store

```typescript
// app.module.ts

import { StoreModule } from '@ngrx/store';

import { counterReducer } from './counter.reducer';

@NgModule({

imports: [

StoreModule.forRoot({ counter: counterReducer }),

//...

],
```

```typescript
})

export class AppModule {}
```

2.4. Using the Store in a Component

```typescript
// counter.component.ts

import { Component } from '@angular/core';

import { Store, select } from '@ngrx/store';

import { increment, decrement } from './counter.actions';

@Component({

selector: 'app-counter',

template: `

<p>Count: {{ count$ | async }}</p>

<button (click)="increment()">Increment</button>

<button (click)="decrement()">Decrement</button>

`,

})

export class CounterComponent {

count$ = this.store.pipe(select('counter'));

constructor(private store: Store) {}

increment() {

this.store.dispatch(increment());
```

```
}

decrement() {

this.store.dispatch(decrement());

}

}
```

3. Conclusion

Angular offers multiple options for managing state in your applications. You can start with Angular services for simpler state management needs, and as your application grows in complexity, consider using libraries like NgRx to handle advanced state management tasks. Choosing the right approach depends on your project requirements and the level of control and scalability you need for your application's state.

7.4 Vue.js and State Management

Vue.js is a progressive JavaScript framework that excels in building user interfaces. When it comes to state management in Vue applications, you have several options. In this section, we'll explore some of these options, including the built-in reactivity system, Vuex for centralized state management, and Composition API for more flexible state handling.

1. Vue's Reactivity System

Vue's core strength lies in its reactivity system, which allows you to create responsive and dynamic user interfaces. Vue automatically tracks changes to data and updates the DOM accordingly.

1.1. Using Vue's Data Property

```
<template>

<div>

<p>Count: {{ count }}</p>

<button @click="increment">Increment</button>

<button @click="decrement">Decrement</button>

</div>

</template>

<script>

export default {

data() {

return {

count: 0,

};

},

methods: {

increment() {

this.count++;

},

decrement() {
```

```
    this.count—;
    },
  },
};
</script>
```

In this example, the count property is automatically reactive, and any changes to it will trigger updates in the template.

2. Vuex for Centralized State Management

For larger Vue.js applications with complex state management needs, Vuex is a popular choice. Vuex provides a centralized store for managing state and actions.

2.1. Setting Up Vuex

First, install Vuex:

```
npm install vuex
```

2.2. Creating a Vuex Store

```
// store.js

import Vue from 'vue';

import Vuex from 'vuex';

Vue.use(Vuex);

export default new Vuex.Store({
```

```
state: {

count: 0,

},

mutations: {

increment(state) {

state.count++;

},

decrement(state) {

state.count—;

},

},

actions: {

increment(context) {

context.commit('increment');

},

decrement(context) {

context.commit('decrement');

},

},

});
```

2.3. *Using Vuex in a Component*

```
<template>

<div>

<p>Count: {{ count }}</p>

<button @click="increment">Increment</button>

<button @click="decrement">Decrement</button>

</div>

</template>

<script>

import { mapState, mapActions } from 'vuex';

export default {

computed: mapState(['count']),

methods: mapActions(['increment', 'decrement']),

};

</script>
```

In this example, we use mapState and mapActions from Vuex to easily connect the component to the Vuex store.

3. Composition API for Flexible State Handling

The Composition API is an addition to Vue.js that provides more flexibility in managing state and logic.

3.1. Using the Composition API

```
<template>

<div>

<p>Count: {{ count }}</p>

<button @click="increment">Increment</button>

<button @click="decrement">Decrement</button>

</div>

</template>

<script>

import { ref } from 'vue';

export default {

setup() {

const count = ref(0);

const increment = () => {

count.value++;

};

const decrement = () => {

count.value—;

};

return {
```

```
      count,

      increment,

      decrement,

    };

  },

};
```

</script>

In this example, we use the Composition API's ref function to create reactive variables and return them from the setup function.

4. Conclusion

Vue.js provides a range of options for state management, from its built-in reactivity system to Vuex for centralized store management and the Composition API for flexible state handling. The choice of state management approach depends on the complexity of your application and your preferences as a developer. Vue's flexibility allows you to select the most suitable method for your project's needs.

7.5 React State and Hooks

React, one of the most popular JavaScript libraries for building user interfaces, offers a powerful way to manage state in your web applications. In this section, we'll explore how to manage state in React applications using the built-in state management system and React Hooks.

1. React's Built-in State Management

React components can manage their internal state using the useState hook. This hook allows you to add state to functional components.

1.1. Using the useState Hook

```typescript
import React, { useState } from 'react';

function Counter() {

const [count, setCount] = useState(0);

const increment = () => {

setCount(count + 1);

};

const decrement = () => {

setCount(count - 1);

};

return (

<div>

<p>Count: {count}</p>

<button onClick={increment}>Increment</button>

<button onClick={decrement}>Decrement</button>

</div>

);
```

```
}
```

export default Counter;

In this example, we use the useState hook to create a count state variable and functions to update it. When setCount is called with a new value, it triggers a re-render of the component with the updated state.

2. Custom Hooks for Reusable State Logic

To share and reuse state logic across components, you can create custom hooks. Custom hooks encapsulate state and behavior, making it easy to share them between different parts of your application.

2.1. Creating a Custom Hook

```
import { useState } from 'react';

function useCounter(initialValue = 0) {

const [count, setCount] = useState(initialValue);

const increment = () => {

setCount(count + 1);

};

const decrement = () => {

setCount(count - 1);

};

return { count, increment, decrement };
```

```
}
```

export default useCounter;

2.2. *Using the Custom Hook*

```
import React from 'react';

import useCounter from './useCounter';

function Counter() {

const { count, increment, decrement } = useCounter();

return (

<div>

<p>Count: {count}</p>

<button onClick={increment}>Increment</button>

<button onClick={decrement}>Decrement</button>

</div>

);

}
```

export default Counter;

By creating custom hooks like useCounter, you can reuse state logic across multiple components.

3. Context API for Global State

For global state management in React applications, you can use the Context API. Context provides a way to share state between components without having to pass props through the component tree manually.

3.1. Creating a Context

```
import React, { createContext, useContext, useState } from 'react';

const CounterContext = createContext();

export function CounterProvider({ children }) {

const [count, setCount] = useState(0);

const increment = () => {

setCount(count + 1);

};

const decrement = () => {

setCount(count - 1);

};

return (

<CounterContext.Provider value={{ count, increment, decrement }}>

{children}

</CounterContext.Provider>
```

```tsx
);
}

export function useCounterContext() {

return useContext(CounterContext);

}
```

3.2. Using the Context

```tsx
import React from 'react';

import { useCounterContext } from './CounterContext';

function Counter() {

const { count, increment, decrement } = useCounterContext();

return (

<div>

<p>Count: {count}</p>

<button onClick={increment}>Increment</button>

<button onClick={decrement}>Decrement</button>

</div>

);
}

export default Counter;
```

By using the Context API, you can share state and functions across different parts of your application.

4. Conclusion

React offers versatile ways to manage state in your applications, whether through its built-in useState hook, custom hooks for reusable state logic, or the Context API for global state management. The choice of state management approach depends on the complexity and requirements of your application. React's flexibility allows you to select the most appropriate method for your project's needs.

Chapter 8: Routing and Navigation

8.1 Implementing Routing in Single-Page Applications

Routing is a fundamental aspect of single-page applications (SPAs) that allows you to navigate between different views or components without the need for full page reloads. In this section, we'll explore how to implement routing in SPAs using popular JavaScript frameworks: Angular, React, and Vue.js.

1. Angular Routing

Angular provides a powerful routing module that enables you to set up and manage routing in your application. Here's a basic example of implementing routing in Angular:

1.1. Setting Up Angular Router

First, install Angular Router:

```
ng add @angular/router
```

1.2. Creating Routes

Define your routes in an Angular module:

```ts
// app-routing.module.ts

import { NgModule } from '@angular/core';

import { RouterModule, Routes } from '@angular/router';

import { HomeComponent } from './home.component';
```

```
import { AboutComponent } from './about.component';

const routes: Routes = [

{ path: '', component: HomeComponent },

{ path: 'about', component: AboutComponent },

];

@NgModule({

imports: [RouterModule.forRoot(routes)],

exports: [RouterModule],

})

export class AppRoutingModule {}
```

1.3. Using RouterOutlet

In your app component template, use the router-outlet directive to display the routed components:

```html
<!--app.component.html-->

<nav>

<a routerLink="/">Home</a>

<a routerLink="/about">About</a>

</nav>

<router-outlet></router-outlet>
```

Angular's router will handle navigation and display the appropriate component based on the route.

2. React Router

React Router is a popular library for handling routing in React applications. Here's a basic example of implementing routing in React:

2.1. Installing React Router

First, install React Router:

npm install react-router-dom

2.2. Creating Routes

Define your routes using the BrowserRouter and Route components:

```
// App.js

import React from 'react';

import { BrowserRouter, Route, Link } from 'react-router-dom';

import Home from './Home';

import About from './About';

function App() {

return (

<BrowserRouter>

<nav>
```

```
<Link to="/">Home</Link>

<Link to="/about">About</Link>

</nav>

<Route path="/" exact component={Home} />

<Route path="/about" component={About} />

</BrowserRouter>

);

}

export default App;
```

2.3. Using Links and Routes

You can use Link components to navigate between routes and Route components to define what to render for each route.

3. Vue Router

Vue Router is the official routing library for Vue.js applications. Here's a basic example of implementing routing in Vue.js:

3.1. Installing Vue Router

First, install Vue Router:

```
npm install vue-router
```

3.2. Creating Routes

Define your routes in a Vue Router instance:

```
// router.js

import Vue from 'vue';

import VueRouter from 'vue-router';

import Home from './components/Home.vue';

import About from './components/About.vue';

Vue.use(VueRouter);

const routes = [

{ path: '/', component: Home },

{ path: '/about', component: About },

];

const router = new VueRouter({

routes,

});

export default router;
```

3.3. Using <router-view> and <router-link>

In your app component template, use the <router-view> element
to display the routed components, and <router-link> elements to
navigate:

```
<!—App.vue—>

<template>

<div>

<router-link to="/">Home</router-link>

<router-link to="/about">About</router-link>

<router-view></router-view>

</div>

</template>
```

Vue Router handles navigation and component rendering based on the route.

4. Conclusion

Routing is essential for building SPAs, and various JavaScript frameworks provide tools and libraries to make implementing routing straightforward. Whether you're using Angular, React, or Vue.js, understanding and effectively using their routing systems is crucial for creating dynamic and interactive web applications.

8.2 Angular Routing with TypeScript

Angular is a popular JavaScript framework for building single-page applications (SPAs). In the previous section, we introduced the concept of routing in SPAs. Now, let's dive deeper into Angular routing with TypeScript.

1. Setting Up Angular Routing

To get started with Angular routing, you need to set up the Angular Router module and define your routes. Here's a step-by-step guide:

1.1. Install Angular Router

If you haven't already, install the Angular Router module:

```
ng add @angular/router
```

1.2. Define Routes

In your Angular application, you'll define routes using TypeScript. Create a TypeScript file (e.g., app-routing.module.ts) to configure your routes:

```
import { NgModule } from '@angular/core';

import { RouterModule, Routes } from '@angular/router';

// Import your components here

import { HomeComponent } from './home.component';

import { AboutComponent } from './about.component';

const routes: Routes = [

{ path: '', component: HomeComponent }, // Default route

{ path: 'about', component: AboutComponent },

];

@NgModule({
```

imports: [RouterModule.forRoot(routes)],

exports: [RouterModule],

})

export class AppRoutingModule {}

In this example, we've defined two routes: the default route ('') and the 'about' route. When a user navigates to these paths, Angular will display the associated components.

1.3. Add Router Outlet

In your application's main template (e.g., app.component.html), add the <router-outlet></router-outlet> element. This placeholder will be replaced with the component associated with the current route:

<!—app.component.html—>

<nav>

<a routerLink="/">Home**</a>**

<a routerLink="/about">About**</a>**

</nav>

<router-outlet></router-outlet>

Now, when users click on 'Home' or 'About' links, Angular will load the corresponding component and display it within the <router-outlet>.

2. Navigating Between Routes

Angular provides a Router service for navigating between routes programmatically in TypeScript. You can use this service in your components to trigger route changes.

2.1. Inject the Router Service

In the component where you want to perform navigation, inject the Router service in the constructor:

```typescript
import { Component } from '@angular/core';

import { Router } from '@angular/router';

@Component({

selector: 'app-home',

template: `

<h1>Welcome to the Home Page</h1>

<button (click)="navigateToAbout()">Go to About Page</button>

`,

})

export class HomeComponent {

constructor(private router: Router) {}

navigateToAbout() {

this.router.navigate(['/about']);
```

```
}

}
```

In this example, clicking the "Go to About Page" button triggers the navigateToAbout method, which uses the Router service to navigate to the 'about' route.

3. Route Parameters

Angular allows you to define route parameters in your routes. These parameters are placeholders in the route path that can capture dynamic values.

3.1. Define Route with Parameters

```
const routes: Routes = [

{ path: '', component: HomeComponent },

{ path: 'about/:id', component: AboutComponent }, // Route with a parameter

];
```

In this example, we've defined a route with a parameter ':id'. This parameter will capture values from the route URL.

3.2. Accessing Route Parameters

You can access route parameters using the ActivatedRoute service in your component:

```
import { Component } from '@angular/core';

import { ActivatedRoute } from '@angular/router';
```

```typescript
@Component({

selector: 'app-about',

template: `

<h1>About Page</h1>

<p>Parameter Value: {{ paramValue }}</p>

`,

})

export class AboutComponent {

paramValue: string;

constructor(private route: ActivatedRoute) {

this.paramValue = this.route.snapshot.paramMap.get('id');

}

}
```

In this example, we retrieve the 'id' parameter value from the route using ActivatedRoute and display it in the component.

4. Guarding Routes

Angular provides route guards to control access to routes. You can implement guards using TypeScript to protect certain routes from unauthorized access.

4.1. Create a Route Guard

```typescript
import { Injectable } from '@angular/core';
```

```typescript
import {
CanActivate,
ActivatedRouteSnapshot,
RouterStateSnapshot,
Router,
} from '@angular/router';
@Injectable({
providedIn: 'root',
})
export class AuthGuard implements CanActivate {
constructor(private router: Router) {}
canActivate(
next: ActivatedRouteSnapshot,
state: RouterStateSnapshot
): boolean {
// Check if user is authenticated (implement your logic here)
const isAuthenticated = true; // Example: Replace with actual logic
if (isAuthenticated) {
return true; // Allow access to the route
} else {
```

```
this.router.navigate(['/login']); // Redirect to login page

return false; // Block access to the route

}

}

}
```

In this example, we've created an AuthGuard that implements the CanActivate interface. It checks whether the user is authenticated and either allows access to the route or redirects to the login page.

4.2. Apply Guard to a Route

You can apply the guard to a specific route by adding a canActivate property to the route configuration:

```
const routes: Routes = [

{ path: '', component: HomeComponent },

{

path: 'secure',

component: SecureComponent,

canActivate: [AuthGuard], // Apply AuthGuard to this route

},

];
```

Now, the 'AuthGuard' will be executed before the 'secure' route is accessed, ensuring that only authenticated users can access it.

5. Conclusion

Angular routing with TypeScript is a powerful feature for building dynamic single-page applications.

8.3 React Router and TypeScript

React is a popular JavaScript library for building user interfaces, and React Router is the standard routing library for React applications. In this section, we'll explore how to use React Router with TypeScript to implement routing in your React projects.

1. Setting Up React Router

To get started with React Router and TypeScript, follow these steps:

1.1. Install React Router

If you haven't already, you need to install React Router in your project:

npm install react-router-dom

1.2. Define Routes

In a typical React application, you'll define your routes using TypeScript. Here's an example of how you can set up your routes in a TypeScript file (e.g., App.tsx):

import React from 'react';

import { BrowserRouter as Router, Route, Switch } from 'react-router-dom';

// Import your components here

```tsx
import Home from './components/Home';

import About from './components/About';

import NotFound from './components/NotFound';

function App() {

return (

<Router>

<Switch>

<Route path="/" exact component={Home} />

<Route path="/about" component={About} />

<Route component={NotFound} />

</Switch>

</Router>

);

}

export default App;
```

In this example, we've imported the necessary components and used the BrowserRouter, Route, and Switch components from 'react-router-dom' to define our routes.

1.3. Create Route Components

You'll need to create separate components for each route. Here's an example of a simple component for the 'Home' route:

```
import React from 'react';

function Home() {

return (

<div>

<h1>Welcome to the Home Page</h1>

{/* Add your content here */}

</div>

);

}

export default Home;
```

Similarly, you can create components for other routes like 'About' and 'NotFound.'

2. Navigating Between Routes

React Router provides several ways to navigate between routes programmatically in TypeScript.

2.1. Using the Link Component

You can use the Link component to create navigation links. Here's an example:

```
import React from 'react';

import { Link } from 'react-router-dom';

function Navigation() {
```

```
return (

<nav>

<ul>

<li>

<Link to="/">Home</Link>

</li>

<li>

<Link to="/about">About</Link>

</li>

</ul>

</nav>

);

}

export default Navigation;
```

In this example, clicking on the 'Home' or 'About' links will navigate to the respective routes.

2.2. Using the useHistory Hook

You can also use the useHistory hook to programmatically navigate to different routes within your components:

```
import React from 'react';
```

```
import { useHistory } from 'react-router-dom';

function MyComponent() {

const history = useHistory();

const navigateToAbout = () => {

history.push('/about');

};

return (

<div>

<button onClick={navigateToAbout}>Go to About Page</button>

</div>

);

}

export default MyComponent;
```

In this example, clicking the button triggers the navigateToAbout function, which uses the push method from useHistory to navigate to the 'about' route.

3. Route Parameters

React Router allows you to define route parameters in your routes, similar to Angular. Here's how you can work with route parameters in TypeScript:

3.1. Define Route with Parameters

```
<Route path="/user/:id" component={UserProfile} />
```

In this example, we've defined a route with a parameter ':id.' This parameter can capture dynamic values from the route URL.

3.2. Accessing Route Parameters

To access route parameters within your component, you can use the useParams hook:

```
import React from 'react';

import { useParams } from 'react-router-dom';

function UserProfile() {

const { id } = useParams<{ id: string }>();

return (

<div>

<h1>User Profile</h1>

<p>User ID: {id}</p>

</div>

);

}

export default UserProfile;
```

In this example, we use the useParams hook to access the 'id' parameter from the route and display it in the component.

4. Nested Routes

React Router also supports nested routes, allowing you to define routes within routes. This is useful for building complex page layouts with different components.

4.1. Define Nested Routes

```
<Route path="/dashboard">

<Dashboard>

<Route path="/dashboard/profile" component={UserProfile} />

<Route path="/dashboard/settings" component={UserSettings} />

</Dashboard>

</Route>
```

In this example, we've defined nested routes for the 'Dashboard' route. When a user navigates to '/dashboard/profile' or '/dashboard/settings,' the corresponding components will be displayed within the 'Dashboard' component.

5. Conclusion

React Router is an essential tool for managing routing in React applications. By combining it with TypeScript, you can create robust and type-safe routing systems that enhance your React projects' functionality and user experience.

8.4 Vue Router and TypeScript

Vue.js is a progressive JavaScript framework for building user interfaces, and Vue Router is the official routing library for Vue applications. In this section, we'll explore how to use Vue Router with TypeScript to implement routing in your Vue projects.

1. Setting Up Vue Router

To get started with Vue Router and TypeScript, follow these steps:

1.1. Install Vue Router

If you haven't already, you need to install Vue Router in your project:

```
npm install vue-router
```

1.2. Create a Vue Router Instance

In your Vue application, you'll create a Vue Router instance to manage routing. Here's an example of how you can set up your Vue Router instance in a TypeScript file (e.g., router.ts):

```typescript
import Vue from 'vue';

import VueRouter, { RouteConfig } from 'vue-router';

Vue.use(VueRouter);

const routes: RouteConfig[] = [
{
path: '/',
component: () => import('./components/Home.vue'),
},
{
```

```
path: '/about',

component: () => import('./components/About.vue'),

},

{

path: '*',

component: () => import('./components/NotFound.vue'),

},

];

const router = new VueRouter({

routes,

});

export default router;
```

In this example, we've defined routes using RouteConfig objects and created a VueRouter instance with these routes.

1.3. Integrate Vue Router with Vue

To integrate Vue Router with your Vue application, you'll need to import the router instance and use it within your main Vue instance. Here's an example of how you can do that in your main.ts or main.js file:

```
import Vue from 'vue';

import App from './App.vue';
```

```
import router from './router';

new Vue({

render: (h) => h(App),

router, // Add the router instance

}).$mount('#app');
```

Now, your Vue application is ready to use Vue Router for routing.

2. Defining and Using Routes

In a Vue Router-enabled application, you can define your routes and use them in your Vue components. Here's how you can define routes and use them in your components:

2.1. Defining Routes

In the router instance (router.ts), you've already defined your routes. Each route consists of a path and a component that corresponds to a Vue component. You can define more routes as needed for your application.

2.2. Using Routes in Components

To use routes within your Vue components, you can take advantage of Vue Router's built-in features.

For example, you can create navigation links using the <router-link> component:

```
<template>

<div>
```

```
<router-link to="/">Home</router-link>

<router-link to="/about">About</router-link>

</div>

</template>
```

In this example, clicking on the 'Home' or 'About' links will navigate to the respective routes.

To display components for different routes, you can use the `<router-view>` component:

```
<template>

<div>

<router-view></router-view>

</div>

</template>
```

The `<router-view>` component will render the component associated with the current route.

3. Route Parameters

Vue Router allows you to define route parameters in your routes. Here's how you can work with route parameters in TypeScript:

3.1. Define Route with Parameters

```
{

path: '/user/:id',
```

```
component: () => import('./components/UserProfile.vue'),
}
```

In this example, we've defined a route with a parameter ':id.' This parameter can capture dynamic values from the route URL.

3.2. Accessing Route Parameters

To access route parameters within your component, you can use the $route object:

```
<template>

<div>

<h1>User Profile</h1>

<p>User ID: {{ $route.params.id }}</p>

</div>

</template>
```

In this example, we use $route.params.id to access the 'id' parameter from the route and display it in the component.

4. Nested Routes

Vue Router also supports nested routes, allowing you to define routes within routes. This is useful for building complex page layouts with different components.

4.1. Define Nested Routes

```
{
```

```
path: '/dashboard',

component: () => import('./components/Dashboard.vue'),

children: [

{

path: 'profile',

component: () => import('./components/UserProfile.vue'),

},

{

path: 'settings',

component: () => import('./components/UserSettings.vue'),

},

],

}
```

In this example, we've defined nested routes for the 'Dashboard' route. When a user navigates to '/dashboard/profile' or '/dashboard/settings,' the corresponding components will be displayed within the 'Dashboard' component.

5. Conclusion

Vue Router is a powerful tool for managing routing in Vue applications, and when combined with TypeScript, it allows you to build type-safe and efficient routing systems. By following the steps and examples in this section, you can easily integrate Vue Router with TypeScript in your Vue.js projects and create dynamic and responsive web applications.

8.5 Advanced Routing Techniques

In this section, we will explore advanced routing techniques that can enhance your web applications. While basic routing helps you navigate between pages, these techniques enable you to create more dynamic and feature-rich routing systems.

1. Nested Routes and Layouts

Nested routes allow you to create complex layouts by nesting multiple components within a single parent route. This is particularly useful for building dashboards or application layouts with sidebars, headers, and content areas.

```
{

path: '/dashboard',

component: DashboardLayout,

children: [

{

path: 'overview',

component: DashboardOverview,

},

{

path: 'analytics',
```

```
    component: DashboardAnalytics,
  },
 ],
}
```

In this example, the 'Dashboard' route has two nested routes: 'overview' and 'analytics.' Each nested route corresponds to a specific component, allowing you to manage the layout and content separately.

2. Named Routes

Named routes make it easier to generate links to specific routes in your application. Instead of hardcoding URLs, you can use route names, making your code more maintainable.

```
{
  path: '/products/:id',
  name: 'product-details',
  component: ProductDetails,
}
```

With a named route, you can generate a link like this:

```
<router-link :to="{ name: 'product-details', params: { id: 123 }}">Product Details</router-link>
```

3. Redirects

Redirects are useful for guiding users to the correct route. You can set up redirects to ensure that old URLs or common typos automatically lead to the correct page.

```
{

path: '/about-us',

redirect: '/about',

}
```

In this example, if a user tries to access '/about-us,' they will be redirected to the '/about' page.

4. Lazy Loading

Lazy loading is a performance optimization technique that loads components only when they are needed. This reduces the initial bundle size and speeds up the initial page load.

```
{

path: '/lazy',

component: () => import('./LazyLoadedComponent.vue'),

}
```

By using the import() function, you can dynamically load components when the corresponding route is accessed.

5. Guards

Route guards allow you to control access to routes based on certain conditions. There are three types of guards: beforeEach, beforeResolve, and afterEach.

- beforeEach: Used for global navigation guards. You can check if a user is authenticated before allowing access to a route.

```
router.beforeEach((to, from, next) => {

if (to.meta.requiresAuth && !AuthService.isAuthenticated()) {

next('/login');

} else {

next();

}

});
```

- beforeResolve: Similar to beforeEach, but it is called after the route components are resolved.

- afterEach: Called after the route navigation is complete. Useful for tracking page views or performing cleanup tasks.

6. Route Metadata

You can attach custom metadata to routes using the meta property. This is handy for storing information like page titles, breadcrumbs, or access control rules.

```
{

path: '/profile',

component: UserProfile,

meta: {

title: 'User Profile',

breadcrumb: 'Profile',

requiresAuth: true,

},

}
```

With route metadata, you can dynamically update the page title or generate breadcrumbs for your application.

7. Error Handling

Handling route errors gracefully is essential for a smooth user experience. Vue Router allows you to define a catch-all route to handle unexpected routes.

```
{

path: '*',

component: NotFound,

}
```

This route captures any unknown paths and displays a 'Not Found' component, ensuring that users are not left with a blank page.

8. Conclusion

By mastering these advanced routing techniques, you can create more sophisticated and user-friendly web applications. Whether it's building complex layouts, optimizing performance, or enhancing user security, Vue Router provides the flexibility and power to meet your routing needs. Incorporate these techniques into your Vue.js applications to take full advantage of Vue Router's capabilities.

Chapter 9: Styling Web Applications

9.1 CSS Preprocessors with TypeScript

Styling is a crucial aspect of web development, and it plays a significant role in creating visually appealing and user-friendly web applications. While Cascading Style Sheets (CSS) are the standard for styling web pages, managing and maintaining large CSS codebases can become challenging. This is where CSS preprocessors come into play.

CSS preprocessors, such as Sass (Syntactically Awesome Style Sheets) and Less, provide enhanced capabilities for writing and organizing CSS code. They introduce features like variables, nesting, mixins, and functions, which make CSS more maintainable and efficient. In this section, we'll explore how you can use CSS preprocessors, specifically Sass, in conjunction with TypeScript to streamline your styling workflow.

1. Installing Sass

Before using Sass in your TypeScript project, you need to install it. You can do this using npm (Node Package Manager):

npm install sass—save-dev

2. Creating a Sass File

Next, you can create a .scss (Sass) file for your styles. For example, let's create a styles.scss file:

// styles.scss

$primary-color: #007bff;

```scss
.button {

background-color: $primary-color;

color: white;

padding: 10px 20px;

border: none;

cursor: pointer;

&:hover {

background-color: darken($primary-color, 10%);

}

}
```

In this example, we define a primary color variable and use it within the .button class. We also take advantage of Sass's nesting capabilities to define hover styles.

3. Importing Sass in TypeScript

To use the styles defined in your Sass file in your TypeScript components, you need to import the Sass file. You can do this in your TypeScript file like so:

```typescript
import './styles.scss';
```

Now, the styles defined in styles.scss will be applied to the components in the TypeScript file.

4. Compiling Sass

To compile your Sass code into regular CSS, you can use a build tool like Webpack or a task runner like Gulp. Configure your build tool to process .scss files and generate .css files that your web application can use.

5. Benefits of Using Sass with TypeScript

Using a CSS preprocessor like Sass with TypeScript offers several advantages:

- **Maintainability**: Variables and mixins make it easier to manage and update styles.

- **Reusability**: Mixins and functions allow you to reuse styles across different components.

- **Nested Styles**: Sass's nesting feature helps maintain a clear hierarchy in your styles, mirroring the component structure.

- **Type Safety**: Although Sass itself doesn't provide type safety, when used with TypeScript, you can achieve type-safe styling by defining TypeScript interfaces for your styles.

In conclusion, integrating CSS preprocessors like Sass with TypeScript can significantly improve your web application's styling workflow, making it more organized, maintainable, and efficient. It's a powerful combination that many web developers find beneficial when building complex and visually appealing user interfaces.

9.2 CSS-in-JS Approaches

In this section, we'll explore CSS-in-JS, an alternative approach to styling web applications that has gained popularity in recent years. CSS-in-JS allows you to write and manage styles using JavaScript or TypeScript, offering various benefits such as scoped styles, dynamic styles, and improved performance. We'll discuss some of the popular CSS-in-JS libraries and how to use them with TypeScript.

1. What Is CSS-in-JS?

CSS-in-JS is a methodology that enables you to write CSS styles using JavaScript or TypeScript. Instead of defining styles in separate CSS files, you define them inline within your JavaScript or TypeScript code. These styles are then dynamically injected into the HTML document when the component or element is rendered.

2. Benefits of CSS-in-JS

CSS-in-JS provides several advantages:

- **Scoped Styles**: Styles are automatically scoped to the component or element they belong to, reducing the risk of class name collisions and unintended side effects.

- **Dynamic Styling**: You can generate styles dynamically based on component props or application state, allowing for more flexible and interactive designs.

- **Improved Performance**: CSS-in-JS libraries often optimize style injection for better performance, reducing the time it takes to apply styles to the DOM.

- **Type Safety**: When using TypeScript, you can achieve type safety with CSS-in-JS by defining TypeScript types for your styles.

3. Popular CSS-in-JS Libraries

There are several CSS-in-JS libraries available, each with its own syntax and features. Some of the popular ones include:

3.1. styled-components

styled-components[1] is a widely used CSS-in-JS library for React. It allows you to define styles as tagged template literals, making it easy to create reusable components with scoped styles.

import styled **from** 'styled-components';

const Button = styled.button`

background-color: #007bff;

color: white;

padding: 10px 20px;

border: none;

cursor: pointer;

&:hover {

background-color: #0056b3;

}

`;

---

1. https://styled-components.com/

3.2. @emotion/styled

@emotion/styled[2] is another CSS-in-JS library for React. It provides a similar syntax to styled-components and is known for its performance and small bundle size.

```js
import styled from '@emotion/styled';

const Button = styled.button`

background-color: #007bff;

color: white;

padding: 10px 20px;

border: none;

cursor: pointer;

&:hover {

background-color: #0056b3;

}

`;
```

3.3. @mui/styles (Material-UI)

@mui/styles[3] is the styling solution for Material-UI, a popular React UI library. It allows you to create styles using JavaScript objects and provides theming capabilities.

```js
import { makeStyles } from '@mui/styles';
```

---

2. https://emotion.sh/docs/styled

3. https://mui.com/styles/basics/

```typescript
const useStyles = makeStyles((theme) => ({

button: {

backgroundColor: theme.palette.primary.main,

color: 'white',

padding: '10px 20px',

border: 'none',

cursor: 'pointer',

'&:hover': {

backgroundColor: theme.palette.primary.dark,

},

},

}));

function MyButton() {

const classes = useStyles();

return          <button          className={classes.button}>My
Button</button>;

}
```

3.4. *styled-jsx*

styled-jsx[4] is a CSS-in-JS library that works well with Next.js. It allows you to define styles using JSX-style syntax directly within your components.

```
function Button() {

return (

<>

<style jsx>{`

button {

background-color: #007bff;

color: white;

padding: 10px 20px;

border: none;

cursor: pointer;

}

button:hover {

background-color: #0056b3;

}

`}</style>

<button>My Button</button>
```

---

4. https://github.com/vercel/styled-jsx

```
</>

);

}
```

4. Using CSS-in-JS with TypeScript

When using TypeScript with CSS-in-JS, you can leverage TypeScript's type system to achieve type safety in your styles. Many CSS-in-JS libraries provide TypeScript typings out of the box, allowing you to define types for your styled components and props.

For example, with styled-components, you can define types for your styled components as follows:

```
import styled from 'styled-components';

interface ButtonProps {

primary?: boolean;

}

const Button = styled.button<ButtonProps>`

background-color: ${(props) => (props.primary ? '#007bff' : 'transparent')};

color: ${(props) => (props.primary ? 'white' : '#007bff')};

padding: 10px 20px;

border: none;

cursor: pointer;

&:hover {
```

```
background-color: ${(props) => (props.primary ? '#0056b3' :
'#eaeaea')};

}

`;

// Usage

const MyComponent = () => {

return (

<div>

<Button>Default Button</Button>

<Button primary>Primary Button</Button>

</div>

);

};
```

In this example, we define an ButtonProps interface to specify the prop types for the Button component, allowing us to use primary as a prop and achieve type safety.

5. Conclusion

CSS-in-JS is a powerful approach to styling web applications, offering scoped styles,

9.3 Theming and Styling Libraries

In this section, we'll explore theming and styling libraries that can help you maintain a consistent and visually appealing design across your web applications. These libraries provide tools and best practices for managing styles, creating themes, and ensuring a cohesive user interface (UI) across your application.

1. Importance of Theming

Consistent theming is essential for creating a visually appealing and user-friendly web application. A well-thought-out theme can define the overall look and feel of your application, making it easier for users to navigate and interact with your content. Theming also allows you to adapt your application's appearance to different user preferences, such as light and dark modes.

2. Popular Theming and Styling Libraries

2.1. Material-UI

Material-UI[5] is a popular React UI library that provides a comprehensive theming system. It follows the Material Design guidelines and offers pre-built components, a flexible styling solution, and a robust theming API.

To use Material-UI theming, you can define a theme using the createTheme function and customize various aspects of your application's design, such as typography, colors, and spacing:

```
import { createTheme, ThemeProvider } from '@mui/material/styles';

const theme = createTheme({

typography: {

fontFamily: 'Roboto, sans-serif',
```

---

5. https://mui.com/

```javascript
  },
  palette: {
    primary: {
      main: '#007bff',
    },
    secondary: {
      main: '#ff6f61',
    },
  },
});

function App() {
  return (
    <ThemeProvider theme={theme}>
      {/* Your application components */}
    </ThemeProvider>
  );
}
```

Material-UI's theming hyssem allows you to easily swithch between different themes, making it suitable for creating dark mode themes, custom themes, and more.

2.2. Ant Design

Ant Design[6] is another popular React UI library known for its rich set of components and theming capabilities. It provides a powerful theming system through the Less preprocessor, allowing you to customize the look and feel of your application extensively.

Ant Design's theming can be achieved by modifying variables in a custom theme.less file. You can adjust colors, fonts, and other styles to create a unique theme:

@primary-color: #007bff;

@secondary-color: #ff6f61;

// More theme variables...

// Import Ant Design styles

@import '~antd/dist/antd.less';

// Your custom styles

// ...

2.3. Tailwind CSS

Tailwind CSS[7] is a utility-first CSS framework that simplifies the process of creating consistent and responsive designs. While not a theming library in the traditional sense, Tailwind CSS allows you to define and maintain a set of utility classes for styling your UI components.

---

6. https://ant.design/

7. https://tailwindcss.com/

To create a custom theme with Tailwind CSS, you can configure the tailwind.config.js file to define your color palette, typography, spacing, and other design choices:

```js
// tailwind.config.js

module.exports = {

theme: {

extend: {

colors: {

primary: '#007bff',

secondary: '#ff6f61',

},

},

},

// ...

};
```

By customizing the configuration, you can enforce a consistent design language throughout your application.

3. Combining Theming and CSS-in-JS

You can also combine theming libraries with CSS-in-JS solutions like styled-components or @emotion/styled to create a seamless styling experience. These libraries allow you to dynamically adapt your component styles based on the current theme.

For example, with styled-components, you can create styled components that consume theme variables:

```typescript
import styled from 'styled-components';

const Button = styled.button`

background-color: ${(props) => props.theme.primary};

color: white;

padding: 10px 20px;

border: none;

cursor: pointer;

`;

// Usage

function MyButton() {

return (

<ThemeProvider theme={theme}>

<Button>Primary Button</Button>

</ThemeProvider>

);

}
```

In this example, the Button component's background color is dynamically set based on the theme's primary color.

4. Conclusion

Theming and styling libraries are essential tools for maintaining a consistent and visually pleasing design across your web applications. Whether you choose Material-UI, Ant Design, Tailwind CSS, or a combination of these libraries, a thoughtful approach to theming can significantly enhance the user experience and streamline your development process.

9.4 Responsive Design in TypeScript

Responsive design is a critical aspect of modern web development. It ensures that your web applications adapt to various screen sizes and devices, providing an optimal user experience on desktops, tablets, and mobile phones. In this section, we'll explore responsive design techniques in TypeScript and how to create web applications that look and work well across different devices.

1. Understanding Responsive Design

Responsive design is the practice of designing and building web applications to provide an optimal viewing and interaction experience across a wide range of devices and screen sizes. It involves using flexible layouts, fluid grids, and media queries to adjust the presentation of content based on the device's characteristics.

2. Media Queries

Media queries are a fundamental tool in responsive design. They allow you to apply CSS styles based on the device's screen width, height, orientation, and other properties. TypeScript and JavaScript can be used to manipulate styles or behavior in response to media query changes dynamically.

Here's an example of using TypeScript to listen for changes in the viewport width and apply different styles accordingly:

```typescript
const mediaQuery = window.matchMedia('(max-width: 768px)');

function handleMediaQueryChange(event) {

if (event.matches) {

// Apply styles for small screens

} else {

// Apply styles for larger screens

}

}

mediaQuery.addEventListener('change',
handleMediaQueryChange);

// Initial check for the current viewport size

handleMediaQueryChange(mediaQuery);
```

3. Flexbox and Grid Layout

CSS Flexbox and Grid Layout are powerful tools for creating responsive layouts. TypeScript can be used to dynamically adjust the layout and alignment of elements based on the available space. For example, you can use TypeScript to toggle CSS classes to switch between different flexbox or grid configurations:

```typescript
const container = document.querySelector('.flex-container');

const toggleButton = document.querySelector('.toggle-button');
```

```
toggleButton.addEventListener('click', () => {

container.classList.toggle('column-layout');

});
```

In this example, clicking the "toggleButton" will switch the layout between a row and column flex layout.

4. Responsive Images

Loading appropriate images based on the device's screen size and resolution is crucial for optimizing performance and user experience. TypeScript can help determine the appropriate image source to load dynamically.

```
const imageElement = document.querySelector('img');

if (window.innerWidth <= 768) {

imageElement.src = 'small-image.jpg';

} else {

imageElement.src = 'large-image.jpg';

}
```

5. Testing and Debugging

Testing responsive design is essential to ensure your application works as expected on various devices and screen sizes. Consider using browser developer tools to simulate different viewports and test your application's responsiveness thoroughly. Additionally, automated testing tools and services can help identify layout and design issues across multiple devices.

6. Frameworks and Libraries

Many frontend frameworks and libraries, such as React, Angular, and Vue.js, provide built-in support for responsive design. They offer responsive layout components and directives that simplify the implementation of responsive features. Leveraging these tools can significantly reduce the complexity of building responsive web applications.

7. Conclusion

Responsive design is a crucial aspect of modern web development, and TypeScript can play a significant role in creating responsive web applications. By using media queries, flexible layouts, and responsive images, you can ensure that your application looks and functions well on various devices, providing an excellent user experience across the board.

9.5 Debugging and Optimizing Styles

Debugging and optimizing styles in TypeScript web applications are essential for ensuring a smooth user experience and optimal performance. In this section, we'll explore techniques for debugging and optimizing styles in TypeScript projects.

1. Debugging Styles

Using Browser Developer Tools

Browser developer tools are invaluable for inspecting and debugging styles in TypeScript applications. Most modern browsers offer robust developer tools that allow you to inspect HTML elements, view computed styles, and edit CSS in real-time. You can use these tools to identify styling issues, test changes, and debug layout problems.

Using CSS Linters

CSS linting tools like Stylelint can help you maintain consistent and error-free styles in your TypeScript project. These tools analyze your CSS code for potential issues, such as syntax errors, unused selectors, and style rule violations. Integrating a CSS linter into your development workflow can catch problems early and ensure your styles are clean and maintainable.

Adding Debug Styles

In some cases, adding temporary debug styles can help pinpoint styling issues. For example, you can add a red border to an element to identify layout problems:

```css
/* Debug style to highlight layout issues */

.debug-border {

border: 2px solid red !important;

}
```

You can then apply this debug class to problematic elements in your HTML and remove it once you've identified and fixed the issues.

2. Optimizing Styles

Minifying CSS

Minifying your CSS files is a common optimization technique. Minification reduces the file size by removing unnecessary whitespace, comments, and redundant code, making your stylesheets load faster. There are various CSS minification tools available that you can integrate into your TypeScript build process.

Using CSS Sprites

If your application uses multiple small images/icons, consider using CSS sprites. CSS sprites combine multiple images into a single image file, reducing the number of HTTP requests and improving loading times. You can use CSS background-position to display specific parts of the sprite as needed.

Lazy Loading Styles

In some cases, you may want to defer the loading of styles until they are needed. Lazy loading styles can help improve initial page load times. You can achieve this by dynamically adding <link> elements with the rel="stylesheet" attribute to the DOM when specific conditions are met, such as when a user interacts with a particular feature.

Critical CSS

Critical CSS is a technique where you extract and inline the minimal CSS required to render the above-the-fold content of your web page. This ensures that the most important styles load quickly, improving the perceived performance of your application. Tools and services can automate the generation of critical CSS for your pages.

3. Performance Testing

After optimizing your styles, it's crucial to conduct performance testing to assess the impact of your changes. Tools like Google PageSpeed Insights, Lighthouse, and WebPageTest can provide insights into your web application's loading performance and suggest further optimizations.

4. Conclusion

Debugging and optimizing styles in TypeScript web applications are essential steps in delivering a fast and responsive user experience. By using browser developer tools, CSS linters, and optimization techniques like minification and lazy loading, you can ensure that your styles are clean, efficient, and performant. Performance testing tools can help validate the improvements and identify any remaining issues for further refinement.

Chapter 10: Consuming APIs and Web Services

10.1 Making HTTP Requests with TypeScript

Consuming APIs and web services is a common task in web development, and TypeScript provides powerful tools for making HTTP requests to retrieve data from remote servers. In this section, we'll explore how to use TypeScript to make HTTP requests using various methods and libraries.

1. The Fetch API

The Fetch API is a modern JavaScript API for making HTTP requests. It is available in most modern browsers and can be used in TypeScript projects without the need for additional libraries. Here's a basic example of how to make a GET request using the Fetch API:

```typescript
fetch('https://api.example.com/data')

.then((response) => {

if (!response.ok) {

throw new Error(`HTTP error! Status: ${response.status}`);

}

return response.json();
})

.then((data) => {
```

```
// Process the data

console.log(data);

})

.catch((error) => {

console.error('Fetch error:', error);

});
```

In this example, we use the fetch function to make a GET request to the specified URL. We handle the response using promises, checking for errors and processing the data once it's available.

2. Axios

Axios is a popular JavaScript library for making HTTP requests that can be used in TypeScript projects. It provides a more user-friendly API compared to the Fetch API and includes features like request cancellation and automatic JSON parsing. To use Axios, you'll need to install it first:

```
npm install axios
```

Here's an example of making a GET request with Axios:

```
import axios from 'axios';

axios.get('https://api.example.com/data')

.then((response) => {

// Process the data

console.log(response.data);
```

```
})

.catch((error) => {

console.error('Axios error:', error);

});
```

Axios simplifies the process of making HTTP requests and handling responses, making it a popular choice for many TypeScript developers.

3. Axios Interceptors

Axios also allows you to set up interceptors, which are functions that can be executed before a request is sent or after a response is received. Interceptors provide a way to globally handle common tasks like adding headers, logging, or error handling. Here's an example of using Axios interceptors:

```
import axios from 'axios';

// Add an interceptor to set a common header

axios.interceptors.request.use((config) => {

config.headers.common['Authorization'] = 'Bearer your-access-token';

return config;

});

// Add an interceptor to handle errors

axios.interceptors.response.use(

(response) => response,
```

```javascript
(error) => {

console.error('Axios error:', error);

return Promise.reject(error);

}

);

// Make a GET request

axios.get('https://api.example.com/data')

.then((response) => {

// Process the data

console.log(response.data);

});
```

Interceptors allow you to centralize and customize various aspects of your HTTP requests and responses.

4. HttpClient in Angular

If you're using Angular, it provides its own HttpClient module for making HTTP requests. Here's an example of using HttpClient to make a GET request in an Angular component:

```javascript
import { Component, OnInit } from '@angular/core';

import { HttpClient } from '@angular/common/http';

@Component({

selector: 'app-data',
```

```typescript
templateUrl: './data.component.html',

styleUrls: ['./data.component.css']

})

export class DataComponent implements OnInit {

constructor(private http: HttpClient) {}

ngOnInit() {

this.http.get('https://api.example.com/data')

.subscribe((data) => {

// Process the data

console.log(data);

});

}

}
```

Angular's HttpClient module simplifies the process of making HTTP requests in Angular applications.

5. Conclusion

Making HTTP requests to consume APIs and web services is a fundamental part of web development. TypeScript offers various methods and libraries like the Fetch API, Axios, and Angular's HttpClient to streamline this process. Depending on your project's requirements and preferences, you can choose the approach that best suits your needs.

10.2 Fetch API and TypeScript

In the previous section, we explored how to make HTTP requests using the Fetch API in TypeScript. The Fetch API is a modern JavaScript API that provides a straightforward way to send HTTP requests and handle responses. In this section, we'll dive deeper into using the Fetch API with TypeScript and cover common scenarios you might encounter when working with APIs.

1. Making GET Requests

Making a GET request using the Fetch API is relatively straightforward in TypeScript. You can use the fetch function to initiate a GET request and handle the response using promises. Here's a basic example:

fetch('https://api.example.com/posts')

.then((response) => {

if (!response.ok) {

throw new Error(`HTTP error! Status: ${response.status}`);

}

return response.json();

})

.then((data) => {

// Process the data

console.log(data);

})

```
.catch((error) => {

console.error('Fetch error:', error);

});
```

In this example, we make a GET request to retrieve a list of posts from an API. We check the response's status and then parse the JSON response if the request is successful.

2. Making POST Requests

To make a POST request using the Fetch API, you need to provide additional configuration options, such as the request method and the request body. Here's an example of making a POST request with JSON data:

```
const postData = {

title: 'New Post',

body: 'This is the body of the new post.',

};

fetch('https://api.example.com/posts', {

method: 'POST',

headers: {

'Content-Type': 'application/json',

},

body: JSON.stringify(postData),

})
```

```
.then((response) => {

if (!response.ok) {

throw new Error(`HTTP error! Status: ${response.status}`);

}

return response.json();

})

.then((data) => {

// Process the response data

console.log(data);

})

.catch((error) => {

console.error('Fetch error:', error);

});
```

In this example, we specify the request method as 'POST', set the 'Content-Type' header to 'application/json', and provide the JSON data in the request body.

3. Handling Errors

Handling errors is an important part of working with HTTP requests. As shown in the examples above, you can use the catch method to handle errors that occur during the request or response processing. Common errors include network issues, server errors, or failed JSON parsing.

4. Async/Await Syntax

You can also use the async/await syntax in TypeScript to make Fetch API requests more readable and concise. Here's how you can rewrite the GET request example using async/await:

```typescript
async function fetchData() {

try {

const response = await fetch('https://api.example.com/posts');

if (!response.ok) {

throw new Error(`HTTP error! Status: ${response.status}`);

}

const data = await response.json();
// Process the data

console.log(data);

} catch (error) {

console.error('Fetch error:', error);

}

}

fetchData();
```

Using async/await can make your code easier to read and maintain, especially when dealing with multiple asynchronous operations.

5. Conclusion

The Fetch API is a powerful tool for making HTTP requests in TypeScript applications. Whether you're retrieving data from a server, sending data via POST requests, or handling errors, the Fetch API provides a versatile and modern way to interact with APIs and web services. By combining it with TypeScript's strong typing and async/await syntax, you can create robust and reliable applications that consume and interact with external data sources.

10.3 Axios for Data Fetching

While the Fetch API is a great choice for making HTTP requests in TypeScript, you might also consider using Axios, a popular JavaScript library specifically designed for making HTTP requests. Axios simplifies the process of working with APIs and provides features like request and response interceptors, request cancellation, and built-in support for handling JSON responses. In this section, we'll explore how to use Axios for data fetching in TypeScript.

1. Installing Axios

First, you'll need to install Axios in your TypeScript project. You can do this using npm or yarn:

npm install axios

 # or

yarn add axios

Once Axios is installed, you can import it into your TypeScript file:

import axios **from** 'axios';

2. Making GET Requests

Axios provides a simple and concise way to make GET requests. Here's an example of fetching data from an API using Axios:

```typescript
import axios from 'axios';

async function fetchData() {

try {

const response = await axios.get('https://api.example.com/posts');

// Access response data

console.log(response.data);

} catch (error) {

console.error('Axios error:', error);

}

}

fetchData();
```

In this example, we use axios.get to make a GET request and await the response. Axios automatically parses JSON responses, so you can directly access the data using response.data.

3. Making POST Requests

To make a POST request with Axios, you can use the axios.post method:

```typescript
import axios from 'axios';

async function createPost() {
```

```javascript
try {

const postData = {

title: 'New Post',

body: 'This is the body of the new post.',

};

const response = await axios.post('https://api.example.com/posts',
postData);

// Access response data

console.log(response.data);

} catch (error) {

console.error('Axios error:', error);

}

}

createPost();
```

Just like with GET requests, Axios handles the request configuration and response parsing for you.

4. Axios Interceptors

Axios allows you to define interceptors for requests and responses. Interceptors are functions that can be used to modify requests or responses globally. For example, you can use request interceptors to add authentication headers to every outgoing request. Here's a basic example:

```typescript
import axios from 'axios';

// Request interceptor

axios.interceptors.request.use((config) => {

// Modify the request config here (e.g., add authentication headers)

return config;

});

// Response interceptor

axios.interceptors.response.use(

(response) => {

// Modify the response data here

return response;

},

(error) => {

// Handle errors globally

return Promise.reject(error);

}

);
```

5. Conclusion

Axios is a powerful library for making HTTP requests in TypeScript applications. It provides a convenient and expressive API for working with APIs and web services, and its support for interceptors and request cancellation can simplify complex scenarios. Whether you choose Axios or the Fetch API, TypeScript's strong typing and async/await syntax make working with asynchronous HTTP requests more manageable and less error-prone.

10.4 GraphQL and TypeScript

GraphQL is a query language for APIs that allows clients to request exactly the data they need, nothing more and nothing less. It's gaining popularity as an alternative to REST APIs, especially for frontend development. In this section, we'll explore how to work with GraphQL in TypeScript.

1. What is GraphQL?

GraphQL was developed by Facebook and released as an open-source project in 2015. It provides a more efficient and flexible way to request data from servers compared to traditional REST APIs. With GraphQL, clients can specify the shape and structure of the data they need in a single query, reducing over-fetching and under-fetching of data.

Here's a simple example of a GraphQL query:

```
query {
  user(id: 1) {
    id
    name
    email
  }
}
```

```
}
```

This query asks for a user's ID, name, and email. With REST, you might need multiple endpoints to fetch this data, but GraphQL allows you to retrieve it in one request.

2. Setting Up GraphQL Server

To work with GraphQL in TypeScript, you'll need a GraphQL server. Popular options include Apollo Server, Express with express-graphql, and Prisma.

Here's a basic example of setting up an Apollo Server with TypeScript:

```typescript
import { ApolloServer, gql } from 'apollo-server';

const typeDefs = gql`

type Query {

user(id: ID!): User

}

type User {

id: ID!

name: String

email: String

}

`;

const resolvers = {
```

```typescript
Query: {

user: (parent, args, context, info) => {

// Fetch user data from a database or API

return {

id: args.id,

name: 'John Doe',

email: 'john@example.com',

};

},

},

};

const server = new ApolloServer({ typeDefs, resolvers });

server.listen().then(({ url }) => {

console.log(`Server running at ${url}`);

});
```

In this example, we define a simple GraphQL schema with a User type and a user query. The resolver function for the user query fetches user data.

3. Making GraphQL Queries

To make GraphQL queries in TypeScript, you can use libraries like Apollo Client or graphql-request. Apollo Client is a comprehensive

GraphQL client library, while graphql-request is a lightweight alternative.

Here's an example using graphql-request to make a query:

```typescript
import { request, gql } from 'graphql-request';

const query = gql`
query {
user(id: 1) {
id
name
email
}
}
`;

const endpoint = 'https://your-graphql-api.com';

request(endpoint, query)
.then((data) => {
console.log(data.user);
})
.catch((error) => {
console.error('GraphQL error:', error);
});
```

This code sends a GraphQL query to the specified endpoint and retrieves the requested data.

4. GraphQL and TypeScript Typing

One of the advantages of using TypeScript with GraphQL is strong typing. GraphQL schemas provide type information that can be automatically generated as TypeScript types. Tools like graphql-codegen can generate TypeScript typings based on your GraphQL schema, making your frontend code type-safe.

5. Conclusion

GraphQL is a powerful technology for building APIs and fetching data efficiently in TypeScript applications. When combined with TypeScript, it offers a type-safe way to work with data, reducing runtime errors and enhancing developer productivity. Whether you're building a GraphQL server or consuming GraphQL APIs in your frontend, TypeScript's type system and tooling support can greatly improve your development experience.

10.5 Error Handling and Data Transformation

When working with APIs and web services in TypeScript, error handling and data transformation are crucial aspects of ensuring the reliability and stability of your applications. In this section, we'll explore best practices for handling errors and transforming data when dealing with external services.

1. Error Handling

1.1 Handling HTTP Errors

When making HTTP requests in TypeScript, it's important to handle potential errors that can occur during the request. Common HTTP errors include 404 (Not Found), 401 (Unauthorized), 500 (Internal Server Error), and more. Here's an example of how to handle HTTP errors using the axios library:

```typescript
import axios from 'axios';

axios.get('https://api.example.com/data')

.then((response) => {

// Handle successful response

console.log(response.data);

})

.catch((error) => {

// Handle HTTP error

if (error.response) {

console.error(`HTTP error: ${error.response.status}`);

} else if (error.request) {

console.error('Network error: Request failed.');

} else {

console.error('Error:', error.message);
```

```
}
```

```
});
```

In this code, we use the .catch block to handle any errors that may occur during the HTTP request. Depending on the error type, we can differentiate between network errors, server errors, and other types of errors.

1.2 Custom Error Handling

It's a good practice to define custom error classes for specific error scenarios in your application. For example, you can create a custom ApiError class to represent errors from your API:

```
class ApiError extends Error {

constructor(message: string, status: number) {

super(message);

this.name = 'ApiError';

this.status = status;

}

}

// Usage:

try {

// Make API request

} catch (error) {

if (error instanceof ApiError) {
```

```
console.error(`API          Error:          ${error.message}          (Status:
${error.status})`);

} else {

console.error('An unexpected error occurred:', error);

}

}
```

Custom error classes provide better error handling and help you differentiate between different types of errors in your code.

2. Data Transformation

2.1 Normalizing Data

When dealing with data from external services, it's common to normalize the data to ensure consistency and ease of use within your application. Normalization involves converting data into a consistent format or structure. For example, you might convert dates into a standard format, ensure that keys are in camelCase, or remove unnecessary fields.

```
const rawData = {

user_name: 'JohnDoe',

birth_date: '1990-05-15',

// ...

};

const normalizedData = {
```

```
userName: 'JohnDoe',

birthDate: '1990-05-15',

// ...

};
```

Normalizing data simplifies data manipulation and reduces inconsistencies in your application.

2.2 Data Validation and Sanitization

Before using external data in your TypeScript application, it's essential to validate and sanitize the data to prevent security vulnerabilities and unexpected behavior. Libraries like validator can help with data validation, while DOMPurify can assist in sanitizing HTML content to prevent cross-site scripting (XSS) attacks.

```
import validator from 'validator';

const userInput = 'user@example.com';

if (validator.isEmail(userInput)) {

// Valid email address

} else {

// Invalid email address

}
```

3. Conclusion

Effective error handling and data transformation are critical for building robust TypeScript applications that interact with external services. Properly handling errors ensures graceful degradation in the face of unexpected issues, while data transformation helps maintain data consistency and security. By following best practices and using relevant libraries and tools, you can enhance the reliability and security of your TypeScript applications when working with APIs and web services.

Chapter 11: Real-time Applications with WebSocket

Section 11.1: Introduction to WebSockets

WebSockets are a communication protocol that enables real-time, bidirectional, full-duplex communication between a client (usually a web browser) and a server. Unlike traditional HTTP requests that follow a request-response pattern, WebSockets establish a persistent connection between the client and server, allowing them to exchange data in both directions without the overhead of opening and closing connections for each message.

The Need for Real-time Communication

In web applications, there are many scenarios where real-time communication is essential. Consider chat applications, online gaming, collaborative document editing, financial trading platforms, and live sports updates. In all these cases, users expect instant updates and interaction with the application without needing to refresh the page or request data continuously.

Traditional HTTP-based approaches, while suitable for many tasks, have limitations when it comes to real-time communication. They rely on the client sending requests to the server, which responds with updated data. This approach can be inefficient for real-time scenarios as it often involves polling the server at regular intervals, which can lead to unnecessary network traffic and latency.

How WebSockets Work

WebSockets provide a more efficient way to handle real-time communication. Here's how they work:

1. **WebSocket Handshake**: The process begins with a WebSocket handshake. The client sends an HTTP request with an "Upgrade" header indicating its intention to establish a WebSocket connection. If the server supports WebSockets, it responds with an HTTP 101 status code, indicating a successful WebSocket handshake.

2. **WebSocket Connection**: Once the handshake is complete, the connection is upgraded from HTTP to WebSocket. Both the client and server can now send and receive messages at any time without the need for a new HTTP request.

3. **Full-Duplex Communication**: WebSockets allow full-duplex communication, meaning both the client and server can send messages independently without waiting for a response. This bidirectional communication enables real-time updates and interaction.

4. **Data Framing**: Messages sent over a WebSocket connection are framed with a header that contains information about the message type and length. This framing allows the server and client to understand and process messages correctly.

5. **Low Latency**: WebSockets are designed for low-latency communication. The persistent connection eliminates the need for repeated handshakes, reducing network latency.

6. **Keep-Alive**: WebSockets include built-in mechanisms to keep the connection alive, ensuring that it remains open as long as both the client and server want to communicate.

Supported by Browsers and Servers

WebSockets are supported by modern web browsers and widely used in web development. Most web frameworks and libraries offer WebSocket support, making it relatively straightforward to implement real-time features in web applications. Popular WebSocket libraries in TypeScript and JavaScript include "socket.io" and "ws."

In the next sections, we'll explore WebSocket libraries in TypeScript, build a real-time chat application, discuss security considerations, and examine strategies for scaling real-time applications.

Section 11.2: WebSocket Libraries in TypeScript

When working with WebSockets in TypeScript, you have several libraries and frameworks at your disposal that simplify the implementation of real-time features. These libraries provide abstractions and utilities to manage WebSocket connections, handle messaging, and ensure compatibility with various browsers and server platforms.

Here are some popular WebSocket libraries in TypeScript:

1. socket.io

Socket.io[1] is a widely used WebSocket library that provides real-time bidirectional event-based communication. It works seamlessly with

---

1. https://socket.io/

TypeScript and is compatible with both Node.js on the server side and browsers on the client side. Socket.io offers features like automatic reconnection, rooms for broadcasting messages to specific clients, and support for namespaces.

Example of using Socket.io in TypeScript:

```typescript
// Server-side code

import { Server } from "socket.io";

import http from "http";

const server = http.createServer();

const io = new Server(server);

io.on("connection", (socket) => {

console.log("A user connected");

socket.on("chat message", (message) => {

io.emit("chat message", message); // Broadcast the message to all connected clients

});

socket.on("disconnect", () => {

console.log("A user disconnected");

});

});

server.listen(3000, () => {

console.log("Server is running on port 3000");
```

```
});
```

```html
<!—Client-side code—>

<script src="/socket.io/socket.io.js"></script>

<script>

const socket = io();

document.querySelector("form").addEventListener("submit", (e) =>
{

e.preventDefault();

const message = document.querySelector("#message").value;

socket.emit("chat message", message); // Send a message to the server

document.querySelector("#message").value = "";

});

socket.on("chat message", (message) => {

const li = document.createElement("li");

li.textContent = message;

document.querySelector("#messages").appendChild(li);

});

</script>
```

2. ws

ws[2] is a lightweight WebSocket library for Node.js. It is well-suited for server-side WebSocket implementations in TypeScript. While it doesn't offer as many high-level features as Socket.io, it provides a simple and efficient WebSocket server that can be used in TypeScript projects.

Example of using the "ws" library in TypeScript:

```typescript
import WebSocket from "ws";

import http from "http";

const server = http.createServer((req, res) => {

res.writeHead(200, { "Content-Type": "text/plain" });

res.end("WebSocket server");

});

const wss = new WebSocket.Server({ server });

wss.on("connection", (ws) => {

console.log("A user connected");

ws.on("message", (message) => {

// Broadcast the message to all connected clients

wss.clients.forEach((client) => {

if (client !== ws && client.readyState === WebSocket.OPEN) {

client.send(message);

}

});
```

---

2. https://github.com/websockets/ws

```
});

ws.on("close", () => {

console.log("A user disconnected");

});

});

server.listen(3000, () => {

console.log("Server is running on port 3000");

});
```

These are just two examples, and there are more WebSocket libraries available for TypeScript, each with its own set of features and use cases. Depending on your project requirements and familiarity with a specific library, you can choose the one that best fits your needs. WebSocket libraries make it easier to build real-time applications in TypeScript by handling the underlying WebSocket protocol complexities.

Section 11.3: Building a Real-time Chat Application

Building a real-time chat application is a common use case for WebSocket technology, and TypeScript makes it even more robust and maintainable. In this section, we'll walk through the process of creating a simple chat application using TypeScript and WebSockets.

Setting Up the Project

1. **Create a New TypeScript Project**: Start by setting up a new TypeScript project using a tool like npm or yarn. You

can initialize a TypeScript project with the following command:

npm init -y

1. **Install Dependencies**: Install the necessary dependencies for your project, including a WebSocket library. In this example, we'll use the "ws" library for server-side WebSocket handling:

npm install ws

1. **Create Project Structure**: Organize your project by creating directories and files. For simplicity, you can have a structure like this:

chat-app/

├── server.ts

├── client.html

├── package.json

└── tsconfig.json

Server-Side Implementation

Now, let's implement the server-side logic for the chat application. We'll create a WebSocket server that listens for incoming connections and handles messages between clients.

// server.ts

import WebSocket **from** "ws";

```typescript
import http from "http";

import { Server } from "http";

const server: Server = http.createServer((req, res) => {

// Handle HTTP requests if needed

});

const wss = new WebSocket.Server({ server });

wss.on("connection", (ws: WebSocket) => {

console.log("A user connected");

ws.on("message", (message: string) => {

// Broadcast the message to all connected clients

wss.clients.forEach((client) => {

if (client !== ws && client.readyState === WebSocket.OPEN) {

client.send(message);

}

});

});

ws.on("close", () => {
console.log("A user disconnected");

});

});
```

```javascript
const PORT = process.env.PORT || 3000;

server.listen(PORT, () => {

console.log(`Server is running on port ${PORT}`);

});
```

Client-Side Implementation

Next, let's create the client-side HTML file that allows users to send and receive messages.

```html
<!—client.html—>

<!DOCTYPE html>

<html lang="en">

<head>

<meta charset="UTF-8">

<meta name="viewport" content="width=device-width, initial-scale=1.0">

<title>Chat App</title>

</head>

<body>

<h1>Real-time Chat</h1>

<div id="messages"></div>

<input type="text" id="messageInput" placeholder="Type your message">
```

```html
<button onclick="sendMessage()">Send</button>

<script>

const socket = new WebSocket("ws://localhost:3000");

socket.addEventListener("message", (event) => {

const messages = document.getElementById("messages");

const message = document.createElement("div");

message.textContent = event.data;

messages.appendChild(message);

});

function sendMessage() {

const messageInput = document.getElementById("messageInput");

const message = messageInput.value;

socket.send(message);

messageInput.value = "";

}

</script>

</body>

</html>
```

Running the Chat Application

To run the chat application, execute the following steps:

1. **Start the Server**: In your project directory, run the TypeScript server:

npm start

1. **Access the Chat**: Open a web browser and visit http://localhost:3000/client.html. You can open this URL in multiple tabs or devices to simulate multiple users.
2. **Start Chatting**: Type messages in the input field and click "Send." The messages will be sent in real-time to all connected clients.

This example demonstrates the basics of building a real-time chat application using TypeScript and WebSockets. You can further enhance the application with features like user authentication, room support, and message history storage to make it more robust and user-friendly.

Section 11.4: WebSocket Security Considerations

When building real-time applications with WebSocket, it's crucial to consider security to protect your application and users from potential threats. In this section, we'll discuss some essential security considerations when using WebSocket in TypeScript.

1. Secure WebSocket (wss)

By default, WebSocket uses the ws protocol, which is not encrypted. To secure WebSocket communication, you should use the wss protocol, which adds a layer of encryption using TLS/SSL. This ensures that data transmitted between the server and clients is encrypted and secure.

To implement wss, you'll need an SSL certificate for your server. Many hosting providers offer SSL certificates, and you can configure your server to use them.

2. Authentication

Implement user authentication to ensure that only authorized users can access your WebSocket server. When a client connects, you can verify their identity using tokens, cookies, or other authentication mechanisms.

Here's a simplified example of authentication when a client connects:

```
wss.on("connection", (ws: WebSocket, request: http.IncomingMessage) => {

const token = request.headers["authorization"];

if (!validateToken(token)) {

ws.close(401, "Unauthorized");

return;

}

// Continue with the WebSocket connection for authenticated users

});
```

3. Rate Limiting

Implement rate limiting to prevent abuse of your WebSocket server. Limit the number of requests or messages a client can send within a specific time frame. This helps protect your server from denial-of-service (DoS) attacks.

4. Input Validation

Always validate and sanitize data received from clients to prevent malicious input. WebSocket data should be treated with the same caution as any other user input to avoid security vulnerabilities like cross-site scripting (XSS) or injection attacks.

5. Cross-Origin Resource Sharing (CORS)

Consider Cross-Origin Resource Sharing (CORS) settings to control which domains can access your WebSocket server. By default, WebSocket connections may be restricted to the same origin due to browser security policies. Adjust CORS settings as needed to allow specific origins to connect.

6. Message Validation

Validate messages received from clients to ensure they meet the expected format and don't contain malicious content. Use a schema or validation library to enforce message structure and data types.

7. Handling Errors

Implement robust error handling to gracefully handle unexpected situations. Proper error handling can prevent information leakage and keep your WebSocket server secure.

8. Logging and Monitoring

Set up logging and monitoring for your WebSocket server to detect and respond to security incidents promptly. Monitoring tools can help you identify unusual activity and potential threats.

9. Keep Libraries Updated

Regularly update the WebSocket library and other dependencies to patch known security vulnerabilities. Vulnerabilities in libraries can pose significant security risks.

10. Security Auditing

Consider conducting security audits or penetration testing on your WebSocket application to identify and address potential vulnerabilities. Professional security assessments can help ensure the highest level of security.

By following these security considerations, you can build a secure WebSocket application in TypeScript that protects your data and users from potential threats. Security should be an integral part of your real-time application development process.

Section 11.5: Scaling Real-time Applications

Scaling real-time applications built with WebSocket can be challenging, especially when you anticipate a large number of concurrent users. In this section, we'll explore strategies for scaling WebSocket-based applications in TypeScript.

1. Load Balancing

Load balancing is a fundamental technique for distributing incoming WebSocket connections across multiple server instances. By distributing the load, you can ensure that no single server becomes a bottleneck. Popular load balancing solutions for WebSocket applications include NGINX, HAProxy, and cloud-based load balancers provided by hosting providers.

Here's an example NGINX configuration for load balancing WebSocket connections to backend servers:

```
http {

upstream websocket {

least_conn;

server backend1.example.com:8080;

server backend2.example.com:8080;

}

server {

listen 80;

location / {

proxy_pass http://websocket;

proxy_http_version 1.1;

proxy_set_header Upgrade $http_upgrade;

proxy_set_header Connection "upgrade";

}

}

}
```

2. Horizontal Scaling

To handle a higher number of concurrent WebSocket connections, you can horizontally scale your WebSocket servers by adding more server instances. Modern cloud platforms like AWS, Google Cloud, and Azure offer tools for automatic scaling based on traffic.

3. Redis Pub/Sub

Using Redis as a message broker for WebSocket communication can help distribute messages across multiple WebSocket server instances. WebSocket servers can subscribe to channels in Redis, ensuring that messages are broadcasted to all connected clients regardless of which server they are connected to.

Here's a simplified example of using the ioredis library for WebSocket message broadcasting with Redis:

```typescript
import Redis from 'ioredis';

import WebSocket from 'ws';

const redis = new Redis();

const wss = new WebSocket.Server({ port: 8080 });

wss.on('connection', (ws) => {

ws.on('message', (message) => {

// Handle incoming WebSocket messages

// Publish the message to a Redis channel

redis.publish('chat', message);

});

});

// Subscribe to the Redis channel
```

```
redis.subscribe('chat');

redis.on('message', (channel, message) => {

// Broadcast the message to all WebSocket clients

wss.clients.forEach((client) => {

if (client.readyState === WebSocket.OPEN) {

client.send(message);

}

});

});
```

4. State Management

Consider externalizing user and application state from your WebSocket server to a distributed database or caching layer. This approach ensures that all WebSocket server instances can access the same state information, enabling seamless communication.

5. Serverless Architectures

Serverless platforms like AWS Lambda or Azure Functions can be used to handle WebSocket connections. These platforms automatically scale based on demand, making them suitable for applications with unpredictable traffic patterns.

6. Monitoring and Auto-Scaling

Implement robust monitoring and alerting to detect traffic spikes and server performance issues. Set up auto-scaling rules to automatically add or remove WebSocket server instances based on predefined criteria, such as CPU utilization or connection count.

7. WebSockets Over HTTP/2

Consider using WebSocket over HTTP/2, which offers improved multiplexing and compression. HTTP/2 can reduce the overhead of WebSocket connections, making it more efficient in handling a large number of simultaneous connections.

8. Database Sharding

If your application relies on databases, database sharding can help distribute the database load by splitting data across multiple database instances. This can improve database performance and reduce contention.

Scaling real-time applications with WebSocket in TypeScript requires careful planning and architecture design. Depending on your application's specific requirements and expected traffic, you may need to combine multiple scaling strategies to ensure seamless and responsive real-time communication for your users.

Chapter 12: Testing and Debugging

Section 12.1: Unit Testing in TypeScript

Unit testing is a crucial aspect of software development that helps ensure the reliability and correctness of your TypeScript code. In this section, we'll delve into unit testing in TypeScript, exploring tools and techniques to write effective unit tests for your applications.

What Is Unit Testing?

Unit testing is the practice of testing individual units or components of your code in isolation. These units can be functions, classes, or even smaller parts of your codebase. The primary goal of unit testing is to verify that each unit of your code works as expected and produces the correct output for a given set of inputs.

Benefits of Unit Testing

Unit testing offers several benefits to developers and software projects:

1. **Early Detection of Issues:** Unit tests can catch bugs and issues early in the development process, making them easier and cheaper to fix.
2. **Improved Code Quality:** Writing unit tests often leads to more modular and maintainable code, as it encourages developers to structure their code in a testable manner.
3. **Regression Testing:** Unit tests serve as a safety net to catch regressions when new code changes are introduced.
4. **Documentation:** Unit tests can act as documentation by providing examples of how code should be used.

Testing Frameworks for TypeScript

To get started with unit testing in TypeScript, you can choose from various testing frameworks. Some popular ones include:

- **Jest:** A widely used JavaScript testing framework that works seamlessly with TypeScript. It offers features like test runners, assertions, and mocking capabilities.

- **Mocha:** A flexible testing framework that can be used with various assertion libraries. It requires additional setup for TypeScript support.

- **Jasmine:** A behavior-driven development (BDD) framework that can be used with TypeScript but requires additional configuration.

- **AVA:** A minimalistic and fast testing framework that also supports TypeScript out of the box.

Setting Up a Testing Environment

To set up a testing environment for your TypeScript project, you'll need to install a testing framework and any additional libraries you plan to use. For example, if you choose Jest, you can install it and related TypeScript dependencies like so:

npm install—save-dev jest @types/jest ts-jest

Next, you'll need to configure your project to use Jest. This typically involves creating a jest.config.js file with the necessary settings.

Writing Your First Unit Test

Let's start with a simple example of writing a unit test for a TypeScript function. Suppose you have the following TypeScript function that adds two numbers:

// *math.ts*

export function add(a: number, b: number): number {

return a + b;

}

You can write a unit test for this function using Jest:

// *math.test.ts*

import { add } **from** './math';

test('add function adds two numbers correctly', () => {

expect(add(1, 2)).toBe(3);

expect(add(-1, 1)).toBe(0);

expect(add(0, 0)).toBe(0);

});

In this example, we import the add function from our math.ts module and use Jest's test function to define a test case. Inside the test case, we use the expect function to make assertions about the behavior of the add function.

Running Tests

You can run your tests using the jest command in your terminal. Jest will discover and execute all test files in your project.

npx jest

Conclusion

Unit testing is a critical practice in software development that helps ensure code quality and maintainability. In this section, we introduced the concept of unit testing and discussed setting up a testing environment for TypeScript projects. We also provided a simple example of writing and running unit tests using the Jest testing framework. In the following sections, we will explore more advanced testing techniques and tools for debugging TypeScript applications.

Section 12.2: End-to-End Testing with TypeScript

End-to-end (E2E) testing is an essential part of ensuring the functionality and user experience of your web applications. In this section, we'll explore E2E testing in TypeScript, discussing tools, frameworks, and best practices for testing your applications from the user's perspective.

What Is End-to-End Testing?

End-to-end testing is a type of testing that simulates a real user's interaction with your application. It involves testing the entire application flow, from the user interface (UI) to the backend, to ensure that the application works as expected. E2E tests help identify issues that may not be caught by unit tests or integration tests.

Benefits of End-to-End Testing

End-to-end testing offers several advantages:

1. **Real User Scenarios:** E2E tests mimic real user interactions, helping discover issues that users might encounter.
2. **Comprehensive Coverage:** E2E tests cover the entire application, ensuring that all components work together correctly.
3. **Integration Verification:** E2E tests can verify that different parts of the application integrate seamlessly.
4. **Regression Detection:** Like unit tests, E2E tests can catch regressions when new code changes are introduced.

E2E Testing Frameworks for TypeScript

Several E2E testing frameworks and libraries are compatible with TypeScript. Some popular choices include:

- **Cypress:** A JavaScript-based E2E testing framework that is highly extensible and easy to set up with TypeScript.

- **Playwright:** A Node.js library that provides cross-browser E2E testing capabilities and native TypeScript support.

- **TestCafe:** A pure Node.js E2E testing framework that can run tests in multiple browsers and supports TypeScript.

Setting Up an E2E Testing Environment

To set up an E2E testing environment for your TypeScript project, you'll need to choose an E2E testing framework, install it, and configure it for TypeScript support.

For example, if you're using Cypress, you can install it and related TypeScript dependencies like this:

npm install—save-dev cypress @types/cypress

You can then initialize Cypress in your project and create your first E2E test spec file.

npx cypress open

Writing Your First E2E Test

Let's create a simple example of an E2E test using Cypress. Suppose you have a web application with a login page. You can write a test to ensure that the login functionality works correctly:

// cypress/integration/login.spec.ts

describe('Login', () => {

it('should log in with valid credentials', () => {

cy.visit('/login'); *// Visit the login page*

cy.get('input[name="username"]').type('user123'); *// Type the username*

cy.get('input[name="password"]').type('password123'); *// Type the password*

cy.get('button[type="submit"]').click(); *// Click the login button*

```
// Assert that the user is redirected to the dashboard

cy.url().should('include', '/dashboard');

});

it('should display an error message for invalid credentials', () => {

cy.visit('/login'); // Visit the login page

cy.get('input[name="username"]').type('invaliduser'); // Type an invalid username

cy.get('input[name="password"]').type('invalidpassword'); // Type an invalid password

cy.get('button[type="submit"]').click(); // Click the login button

// Assert that an error message is displayed

cy.get('.error-message').should('be.visible');

});

});
```

In this example, we use Cypress commands to visit the login page, interact with the UI elements, and make assertions about the application's behavior.

Running E2E Tests

You can run your E2E tests using the Cypress test runner. After initializing Cypress, use the following command:

```
npx cypress run
```

Cypress will open a test runner that allows you to interactively run and debug your E2E tests.

Conclusion

End-to-end testing is crucial for ensuring that your web applications work as expected from the user's perspective. In this section, we introduced the concept of E2E testing and discussed setting up an E2E testing environment in TypeScript. We also provided a simple example of writing E2E tests using the Cypress testing framework. In the following sections, we will explore more advanced testing and debugging techniques for TypeScript applications.

Section 12.3: Debugging TypeScript Applications

Debugging is a crucial skill for developers, as it allows you to identify and fix issues in your TypeScript applications. In this section, we will explore various techniques and tools for debugging TypeScript code effectively.

Debugging Tools

1. Browser Developer Tools: Most modern web browsers come with built-in developer tools that include debugging capabilities. You can set breakpoints, inspect variables, and step through your TypeScript code line by line.

2. Visual Studio Code (VS Code): If you're using VS Code as your code editor, it provides excellent debugging support for TypeScript. You can set breakpoints, use the debugging sidebar, and inspect variables while debugging.

3. Node.js Inspector: When working with TypeScript on the server-side using Node.js, you can use the Node.js Inspector to debug your code. It allows you to attach a debugger to your Node.js process and inspect your server-side TypeScript code.

4. Debugger Statements: You can insert debugger; statements directly into your TypeScript code to create breakpoints. When the code is executed, it will pause at these points, and you can inspect the runtime state.

Debugging Process

Here's a general process for debugging TypeScript applications:

1. **Reproduce the Issue:** Start by reproducing the issue or error in your application. Ensure you can trigger the problem consistently.
2. **Set Breakpoints:** Identify the part of your code where the issue occurs and set breakpoints there. You can set breakpoints in your IDE or code editor.
3. **Start Debugging:** Launch your application in debugging

mode. This may involve running it with specific debugging flags or using a debugger-specific command.

4. **Step Through Code:** Once the debugger pauses at a breakpoint, you can step through the code line by line. You can inspect variables, evaluate expressions, and understand the flow of your program.

5. **Console Logging:** Sometimes, adding console.log statements can be a quick way to debug issues. You can log variable values, messages, or other relevant information to the console to understand what's happening in your code.

6. **Fix the Issue:** Once you've identified the problem, make the necessary code changes to fix it. Test your changes to ensure they resolve the issue.

7. **Regression Testing:** After fixing the issue, run additional tests to ensure that your changes didn't introduce new problems.

Example Debugging Scenario

Suppose you have a TypeScript function that calculates the sum of two numbers but seems to be producing incorrect results. Here's how you can debug it:

```typescript
function add(a: number, b: number): number {

debugger; // Set a breakpoint

const result = a + b;

return result;

}

const sum = add(5, 10);
```

console.log(sum); // *Expected output: 15*

In this example, we've inserted a debugger; statement to set a breakpoint within the add function. When you run this code in a debugger environment, it will pause execution at the debugger; line, allowing you to inspect the values of a, b, and result to identify any issues.

Conclusion

Debugging TypeScript applications is a fundamental skill for developers. By using the right tools and following a systematic debugging process, you can efficiently locate and resolve issues in your code. Remember to test your fixes thoroughly and use debugging as a learning opportunity to understand your code better.

Section 12.4: Profiling and Performance Tuning

Profiling and performance tuning are essential aspects of developing high-quality TypeScript applications. In this section, we will explore how to identify performance bottlenecks and optimize your code for better execution speed and efficiency.

Profiling Tools

1. Browser DevTools: Most web browsers come with built-in profiling tools that allow you to analyze the runtime performance of your JavaScript and TypeScript code. You can use these tools to capture performance profiles, view flame charts, and identify bottlenecks.

2. Node.js Profiler: When working with TypeScript on the server-

side using Node.js, you can use Node.js's built-in profiler to analyze the CPU and memory usage of your application. It generates CPU and heap profiles that help you pinpoint performance issues.

3. Third-Party Profiling Tools: There are third-party profiling tools and libraries available that offer advanced profiling and performance analysis capabilities. Some popular options include Chrome DevTools, Webpack Bundle Analyzer, and Lighthouse.

Profiling Process

Here's a general process for profiling and optimizing TypeScript applications:

1. **Identify the Performance Issue:** Begin by identifying the specific performance issue you want to address. This could be slow page load times, high CPU usage, or excessive memory consumption.
2. **Capture a Performance Profile:** Use the appropriate profiling tool to capture a performance profile while running your TypeScript application. This profile will provide detailed information about the execution of your code.
3. **Analyze the Profile:** Examine the captured profile to identify performance bottlenecks. Look for functions or code sections that consume a significant amount of CPU time or memory.
4. **Optimize the Code:** Once you've identified the problematic code, focus on optimizing it. This may involve refactoring, reducing unnecessary computations, or improving algorithm efficiency.
5. **Reprofile:** After making optimizations, capture another performance profile to assess the impact of your changes.

Ensure that the performance has improved as expected.

6. **Repeat as Needed:** Profiling and optimization are iterative processes. You may need to repeat the steps above multiple times to achieve the desired level of performance.

Example Profiling Scenario

Suppose you have a TypeScript function that performs a computationally expensive operation, and you want to optimize it:

```typescript
function computeFactorial(n: number): number {

if (n <= 1) {

return 1;

} else {

return n * computeFactorial(n - 1);

}

}

const result = computeFactorial(20);

console.log(result);
```

In this example, the computeFactorial function calculates the factorial of a number using a recursive algorithm. However, this recursive approach can be slow for large values of n. To optimize it, you could implement an iterative solution or use memoization to store previously computed values.

Conclusion

Profiling and performance tuning are critical for ensuring that your TypeScript applications run efficiently. By using profiling tools to identify bottlenecks and following a systematic optimization process, you can significantly improve the performance of your code. Keep in mind that performance optimization is an ongoing effort, and it's important to regularly profile and fine-tune your applications as they evolve.

Section 12.5: Continuous Integration and Deployment

Continuous Integration (CI) and Continuous Deployment (CD) are crucial practices in modern software development that enable teams to automate and streamline the process of building, testing, and deploying TypeScript applications. In this section, we'll explore how to set up CI/CD pipelines for your TypeScript projects.

Understanding CI/CD

Continuous Integration (CI):

CI is the practice of regularly integrating code changes from multiple contributors into a shared repository. With CI, every code change triggers an automated build and a suite of tests to ensure that the new code doesn't introduce bugs or regressions. CI helps maintain code quality and consistency by catching issues early in the development process.

Continuous Deployment (CD):

CD takes CI a step further by automating the deployment of code changes to production or staging environments after passing the CI pipeline. CD pipelines typically include additional steps, such as deploying to various environments, running integration tests, and monitoring deployment success.

Setting Up CI/CD for TypeScript

Here's a high-level overview of the steps involved in setting up CI/CD for a TypeScript project:

1. **Version Control:** Ensure your TypeScript project is hosted in a version control system (e.g., Git) and that you have a centralized repository where all contributors push their code changes.
2. **CI/CD Service:** Choose a CI/CD service that integrates with your version control system. Popular options include GitHub Actions, GitLab CI/CD, Travis CI, CircleCI, and Jenkins.
3. **CI Configuration:** Create a configuration file for your chosen CI/CD service (e.g., .github/workflows/main.yml for GitHub Actions) that defines the CI/CD pipeline. This configuration specifies when and how the CI/CD service should build, test, and deploy your TypeScript application.
4. **Automated Builds:** Configure your CI pipeline to automatically build your TypeScript code when changes are pushed to the repository. Ensure that dependencies are installed and that the TypeScript code is transpiled.
5. **Automated Tests:** Set up automated tests that run as part of the CI pipeline. These tests should cover unit tests,

integration tests, and any other relevant tests for your application. Ensure that the CI pipeline fails if any tests fail.

6. **Code Quality Checks:** Consider including code quality checks, such as code linting and static analysis, in your CI pipeline to enforce coding standards and catch potential issues.

7. **Artifact Generation:** If your application produces artifacts (e.g., compiled JavaScript files, assets, or build artifacts), ensure that these artifacts are generated and stored as part of the CI process.

8. **Deployment:** If you're implementing Continuous Deployment, configure your CD pipeline to automatically deploy the application to the desired environment (e.g., staging or production) after a successful CI build and test phase.

9. **Monitoring and Notifications:** Implement monitoring and notification mechanisms to keep the development team informed about the status of CI/CD pipelines. Set up alerts for failed builds or deployments.

10. **Rollbacks:** Plan for rollbacks in case a deployment to production introduces critical issues. CD pipelines should have rollback procedures in place to quickly revert to a stable version.

Example CI/CD Configuration (GitHub Actions)

Here's a simplified example of a GitHub Actions configuration (.github/workflows/main.yml) for a TypeScript project:

```
name: CI/CD Pipeline

on:
```

```
push:

branches:

- main

jobs:

build:

runs-on: ubuntu-latest

steps:

- name: Checkout code

uses: actions/checkout@v2

- name: Set up Node.js

uses: actions/setup-node@v2

with:

node-version: 14

- name: Install dependencies

run: npm install

- name: Build TypeScript

run: npm run build

- name: Run tests

run: npm test
```

This example triggers the CI pipeline on pushes to the main branch, checks out the code, installs Node.js and project dependencies, builds the TypeScript code, and runs tests. A real-world CI/CD configuration would also include deployment steps, notification settings, and additional checks for code quality and security.

Conclusion

Implementing CI/CD for TypeScript projects significantly improves development efficiency, code quality, and deployment reliability. By automating repetitive tasks and ensuring that every code change is thoroughly tested, you can deliver high-quality software with confidence and speed. Choose the CI/CD tools and services that best fit your project's requirements, and continuously refine your CI/CD pipeline to meet evolving needs.

Chapter 13: Authentication and Authorization

Section 13.1: User Authentication Strategies

User authentication is a fundamental aspect of web applications, ensuring that only authorized users can access certain resources or perform specific actions. In this section, we will explore various user authentication strategies commonly used in TypeScript applications.

What is User Authentication?

User authentication is the process of verifying the identity of users before granting them access to protected resources or functionalities. It involves confirming that the user is who they claim to be, typically by requiring them to provide valid credentials such as a username and password.

Common User Authentication Strategies

1. Username and Password Authentication:

- This is the most common form of authentication, where users provide a username and password during login.

- Passwords should be securely hashed and stored in the database to protect user credentials.

- Password-based authentication is suitable for most web applications but requires careful handling of password storage.

2. OAuth and OpenID Connect:

- OAuth and OpenID Connect are widely used authentication protocols for enabling secure authorization and single sign-on (SSO) across multiple applications.

- OAuth allows third-party applications to access user data without exposing the user's credentials.

- OpenID Connect is built on top of OAuth and adds user authentication capabilities, making it suitable for authentication as well as authorization.

3. Multi-Factor Authentication (MFA):

- MFA enhances security by requiring users to provide multiple forms of verification, such as a password and a one-time code sent to their mobile device.

- MFA adds an extra layer of protection against unauthorized access, especially for sensitive applications.

4. Biometric Authentication:

- Some modern devices and applications support biometric authentication methods, such as fingerprint or facial recognition.

- Biometrics provide convenient and secure ways to verify a user's identity.

5. JSON Web Tokens (JWT):

- JWT is a compact, self-contained way to represent user authentication information as a JSON object.

- They are often used for stateless authentication and authorization, where the token contains user claims and can be validated without server-side storage.

Choosing the Right Authentication Strategy

The choice of authentication strategy depends on your application's requirements and security considerations. Here are some factors to consider when selecting an authentication strategy:

- **Security Requirements:** Consider the sensitivity of the data and functionalities in your application. Highly sensitive applications may require stronger authentication methods like MFA.

- **User Experience:** Evaluate the user experience implications of your chosen authentication method. Some methods, like biometric authentication, can provide a seamless and user-friendly experience.

- **Integration:** If your application interacts with external services or APIs, OAuth or OpenID Connect may be the best choice to enable secure integration.

- **Compliance:** Ensure that your authentication strategy complies with relevant data protection and privacy regulations, such as GDPR.

- **Scalability:** Consider how your chosen method scales as your user base grows. Scalability is important for maintaining application performance.

Implementing User Authentication

The implementation of user authentication varies depending on the chosen strategy. Typically, you'll need to:

- **Collect User Credentials:** For username and password authentication, create a user interface for collecting and securely transmitting user credentials.

- **Store User Data:** Safely store user data, including hashed passwords, in a database.

- **Implement Authentication Logic:** Write code to verify user credentials during login and generate authentication tokens or sessions.

- **Integrate Third-Party Services:** When using OAuth or OpenID Connect, integrate with the authentication provider's APIs and implement the necessary flows.

- **Handle MFA:** Implement MFA if required, including mechanisms for sending and verifying one-time codes.

- **Secure JWTs:** If using JWTs, ensure that they are securely generated, signed, and validated to prevent tampering.

- **User Management:** Implement features for user registration, password reset, and account management.

Remember that security is an ongoing process. Regularly update and review your authentication implementation to address new security threats and vulnerabilities.

In the following sections, we will delve deeper into specific authentication and authorization strategies, providing implementation examples and best practices.

Section 13.2: Implementing Authentication in TypeScript

In the previous section, we discussed various user authentication strategies. Now, let's dive into implementing authentication in a TypeScript web application. Authentication is a critical part of securing your application and ensuring that only authorized users can access protected resources.

Authentication Workflow

Authentication typically follows a common workflow:

1. **User Registration:** Users create accounts by providing necessary information such as a username, email, and password. Ensure that passwords are securely hashed before storing them.
2. **User Login:** Users provide their credentials (e.g., username and password) to authenticate themselves.
3. **Authentication Token:** Upon successful login, the server generates an authentication token or session identifier and returns it to the client.
4. **Token Storage:** The client stores this token securely, often in browser cookies or local storage.
5. **Sending Authenticated Requests:** For each request to

protected resources, the client includes the authentication token in the request header.

6. **Token Verification:** The server verifies the token's authenticity and checks if the user has the necessary permissions to access the requested resource.

Libraries and Frameworks

In TypeScript, there are several libraries and frameworks that can simplify authentication implementation:

- **Passport.js:** A popular authentication middleware for Node.js applications that supports various authentication strategies, including username and password, OAuth, and OpenID Connect.

- **jsonwebtoken:** A library for creating and verifying JSON Web Tokens (JWTs), commonly used for stateless authentication.

- **Auth0:** A robust identity platform that provides authentication and authorization as a service. It supports various authentication methods and integrates easily with TypeScript applications.

Example Authentication Implementation

Here, we'll provide a high-level example of implementing username and password-based authentication in a TypeScript application using Node.js and Express.

1. **Set Up Dependencies:**

npm install express passport passport-local passport-local-mongoose express-session

1. Create User Model:

Define a User model with fields like username, email, and hashed password using a library like Mongoose.

1. Configure Passport.js:

Set up Passport.js for handling authentication with the passport-local strategy. Implement serialize and deserialize functions to store and retrieve user information.

1. Routes for Authentication:

Create routes for user registration and login. Handle user registration by creating a new user instance and hashing the password. For login, use Passport.js to authenticate the user.

1. Authentication Middleware:

Implement middleware to check if the user is authenticated before allowing access to protected routes. You can use Passport.js's ensureAuthenticated method.

1. Token Generation (Optional):

If you prefer stateless authentication, you can generate JWTs upon successful login and send them to the client.

1. Secure Storage:

Ensure that sensitive information like passwords and tokens are securely stored and transmitted. Use encryption for sensitive data and HTTPS for secure communication.

1. **Logout:**

Implement a logout route to invalidate the user's session or token and remove it from the client.

1. **Protecting Routes:**

Apply the authentication middleware to routes that require authentication. For example, protecting a route in Express can be done using app.use(ensureAuthenticated).

This is a simplified overview, and real-world implementations should consider additional security measures, such as password hashing with bcrypt, CSRF protection, and secure cookie handling.

Conclusion

Implementing user authentication in TypeScript is a crucial step in securing your web applications. By following best practices, leveraging authentication libraries, and keeping security in mind, you can provide a secure and user-friendly authentication experience for your users.

In the next section, we will explore authorization and role-based access control (RBAC) to further enhance the security of your TypeScript applications.

Section 13.3: Authorization and Role-Based Access Control

In the previous section, we discussed the implementation of user authentication in TypeScript applications. While authentication ensures that users are who they claim to be, authorization is concerned with determining what actions or resources users are allowed to access within the application.

Understanding Authorization

Authorization involves defining and enforcing access control rules based on user roles and permissions. In many applications, users have different roles, such as "admin," "user," or "guest," and each role comes with a set of permissions that determine what actions they can perform and what resources they can access.

Here are some key concepts related to authorization:

- **Roles:** Roles represent a user's category or level within the application. For example, "admin," "editor," and "viewer" are common roles.

- **Permissions:** Permissions specify what actions a user with a particular role can perform. For instance, "create," "read," "update," and "delete" are common permissions.

- **Access Control Lists (ACLs):** ACLs are data structures that define which roles or users have access to specific resources or actions. They help enforce authorization rules.

- **RBAC (Role-Based Access Control):** RBAC is an authorization model that associates roles with permissions. It's a common approach to implementing access control.

Implementing Authorization in TypeScript

To implement authorization in a TypeScript application, you'll need to follow these steps:

1. **Define Roles and Permissions:** Determine the roles and permissions needed for your application. For example, an e-commerce application might have roles like "customer" and "admin" with corresponding permissions.

2. **Associate Roles and Permissions:** Create a mapping that associates roles with the permissions they have. This can be done through code or configuration.

3. **Access Control Logic:** Implement access control logic in your application's routes and controllers. Verify that a user's role allows them to perform a specific action or access a resource.

4. **Middleware:** Use middleware to protect routes and actions that require specific permissions. Middleware can check the user's role and permissions before allowing or denying access.

5. **Authorization Checks:** Perform authorization checks at critical points in your application. For example, when a user tries to edit or delete a resource, ensure they have the necessary permissions.

6. **Error Handling:** Handle unauthorized access gracefully. When a user is denied access, provide informative error messages and responses.

Here's a simplified example of protecting a route in an Express.js application using TypeScript:

```typescript
import express from 'express';

import { checkPermissionMiddleware } from './middleware';

const app = express();

// Define a route that requires admin permissions

app.get('/admin', checkPermissionMiddleware('admin'), (req, res)
=> {

res.send('Admin Dashboard');

});

app.listen(3000, () => {

console.log('Server is running on port 3000');

});
```

In this example, the checkPermissionMiddleware middleware checks if the user has the "admin" role before allowing access to the "/admin" route.

Conclusion

Implementing authorization and role-based access control is essential for securing your TypeScript applications. It ensures that users can only perform actions and access resources that they are authorized to, contributing to the overall security and integrity of your application. In the next section, we will explore OAuth and OpenID Connect as authentication mechanisms in TypeScript applications.

Section 13.4: OAuth and OpenID Connect

with TypeScript

OAuth (Open Authorization) and OpenID Connect (OIDC) are industry-standard protocols for authentication and authorization in web applications. They are widely used to enable secure third-party authentication and single sign-on (SSO) in TypeScript applications. In this section, we'll explore OAuth and OpenID Connect and how to integrate them into your TypeScript projects.

Understanding OAuth and OpenID Connect

- **OAuth:** OAuth is primarily an authorization protocol that allows one application (the client) to access a user's data from another application (the resource server) without revealing the user's credentials. OAuth 2.0 is the most common version used today and is often used for scenarios like allowing a TypeScript app to access a user's Google Drive files or post on their Twitter account without sharing their login credentials.

- **OpenID Connect (OIDC):** OpenID Connect is a layer on top of OAuth 2.0 that adds authentication capabilities. It provides identity verification of the end user by using JSON Web Tokens (JWTs) and allows your TypeScript application to obtain information about the user, such as their username and email address, in a standardized way. OIDC is commonly used for single sign-on (SSO) solutions.

Integrating OAuth and OpenID Connect

To integrate OAuth and OpenID Connect into your TypeScript application, you'll typically follow these steps:

1. **Register Your Application:** First, you'll need to register your TypeScript application with the identity provider (e.g., Google, Facebook, or your organization's OIDC provider). This registration process typically involves obtaining client credentials, such as a client ID and client secret.

2. **Implement OAuth or OIDC Flow:** Depending on your use case and identity provider, you'll choose the appropriate OAuth or OIDC flow. Common flows include the Authorization Code Flow, Implicit Flow, and Hybrid Flow.

3. **Use OAuth Libraries:** There are TypeScript libraries and SDKs available for OAuth and OIDC, such as passport-oauth for Express.js or oidc-client for frontend applications. These libraries simplify the integration process and provide methods for handling authentication and token validation.

4. **Redirects and Callbacks:** Implement redirects and callback routes in your TypeScript application to handle the OAuth or OIDC authentication process. For example, when the user clicks "Sign In," they are redirected to the identity provider's login page. After successful authentication, they are redirected back to your app with an access token or ID token.

5. **Token Validation:** Validate the received tokens on the server-side to ensure their authenticity and to retrieve user information. This step is crucial for security.

6. **User Session Management:** Create and manage user sessions in your TypeScript app to keep users authenticated across multiple requests. You may use cookies or sessions to achieve this.

7. **Logout:** Implement a logout mechanism to clear user

sessions and revoke tokens when the user logs out.

Example OAuth Flow (Express.js)

Here's a simplified example of implementing OAuth using the Passport.js library in an Express.js TypeScript application:

```typescript
import express from 'express';

import passport from 'passport';

import { Strategy as OAuth2Strategy } from 'passport-oauth2';

const app = express();

// Configure Passport to use OAuth2

passport.use(new OAuth2Strategy({

authorizationURL: 'https://oauth-provider.com/auth',

tokenURL: 'https://oauth-provider.com/token',

clientID: 'your-client-id',

clientSecret: 'your-client-secret',

callbackURL: 'http://your-app.com/auth/callback',

}, (accessToken, refreshToken, profile, done) => {

// You can handle user data here and save it to your database

return done(null, profile);

}));

// Route to start the OAuth2 flow
```

```
app.get('/auth/oauth2', passport.authenticate('oauth2'));

// Callback route to handle the OAuth2 response

app.get('/auth/callback', passport.authenticate('oauth2', {
failureRedirect: '/' }), (req, res) => {

// Redirect to the desired page after successful authentication

res.redirect('/profile');

});

app.listen(3000, () => {

console.log('Server is running on port 3000');

});
```

In this example, the application configures Passport to use OAuth2 with an authorization URL, token URL, client ID, and client secret. It then defines routes for starting the OAuth2 flow and handling the callback.

Conclusion

OAuth and OpenID Connect are essential tools for implementing secure authentication and authorization in TypeScript applications. When properly integrated, they allow users to log in with their existing accounts and enable seamless access to protected resources. In the next section, we'll explore security best practices for securing your web applications.

Section 13.5: Securing Your Web Applications

Securing web applications is a critical aspect of software development, as the internet is filled with various security threats and vulnerabilities. In this section, we'll discuss some best practices and techniques for securing your TypeScript web applications.

1. Input Validation

Always validate and sanitize user input to prevent injection attacks like SQL injection and Cross-Site Scripting (XSS). Use libraries and frameworks that offer built-in input validation functions to make this process easier.

```
// Example of input validation using a library like Express-validator

import { body, validationResult } from 'express-validator';

app.post('/signup', [

body('email').isEmail(),

body('password').isLength({ min: 6 }),

], (req, res) => {

const errors = validationResult(req);

if (!errors.isEmpty()) {

return res.status(400).json({ errors: errors.array() });

}

// Continue with user registration

});
```

2. Authentication and Authorization

Implement strong authentication mechanisms to verify the identity of users. Use libraries like Passport.js for authentication and role-based access control for authorization. Ensure that sensitive routes and resources are protected.

3. Session Management

Securely manage user sessions, and avoid storing sensitive data in cookies or client-side storage. Always use secure, HTTP-only cookies for session management and implement mechanisms to regenerate session IDs.

4. HTTPS

Use HTTPS to encrypt data transmitted between the client and server. Obtain SSL/TLS certificates and configure your web server to use HTTPS. Many hosting providers offer free SSL certificates.

5. Content Security Policy (CSP)

Implement a Content Security Policy to mitigate XSS attacks. CSP defines which resources can be loaded by a web page, reducing the risk of executing malicious scripts.

```
<meta http-equiv="Content-Security-Policy" content="default-src 'self'; script-src 'self' 'unsafe-inline'">
```

6. Cross-Site Request Forgery (CSRF) Protection

Protect your application against CSRF attacks by using anti-CSRF tokens and ensuring that state-changing requests require authentication and authorization.

```
// Express.js example using csrf package
```

```
import csrf from 'csurf';

app.use(csrf());

app.get('/form', (req, res) => {

const csrfToken = req.csrfToken();

res.render('form', { csrfToken });

});
```

7. Security Headers

Set security headers in your application to enhance security. Common headers include X-Content-Type-Options, X-Frame-Options, and X-XSS-Protection.

// Example of setting security headers using helmet middleware in Express.js

```
import helmet from 'helmet';

app.use(helmet());
```

8. Error Handling

Implement proper error handling and avoid leaking sensitive information in error messages. Log errors securely and provide user-friendly error pages without revealing internal details.

9. Regular Updates

Keep your dependencies, libraries, and frameworks up to date to patch security vulnerabilities. Use tools like npm audit to identify and fix vulnerabilities.

npm audit

npm audit fix

10. Security Testing

Regularly perform security testing, including penetration testing and code reviews, to identify and mitigate vulnerabilities. Utilize security scanning tools to automate this process.

Conclusion

Securing your TypeScript web applications is an ongoing process that requires vigilance and regular updates. By following these best practices and staying informed about the latest security threats and solutions, you can significantly reduce the risk of security breaches and provide a safer experience for your users. In the next chapter, we'll explore TypeScript in Node.js for server-side development.

Chapter 14: Building Progressive Web Apps (PWAs)

Progressive Web Apps (PWAs) represent a modern approach to building web applications that provide a native app-like experience on the web. PWAs combine the best of both web and native mobile apps, offering features like offline support, push notifications, and fast loading times. In this chapter, we will explore the concept of PWAs and how to build them using TypeScript.

Section 14.1: Understanding PWAs

What is a Progressive Web App (PWA)?

A Progressive Web App (PWA) is a web application that leverages modern web technologies to deliver an enhanced user experience. PWAs are designed to work on any platform that uses a standards-compliant browser, whether it's a desktop computer, tablet, or mobile device. The key characteristics of PWAs include:

1. **Reliability**: PWAs can work offline or in low-network conditions, thanks to service workers and caching strategies. Users can access the app even without a stable internet connection.
2. **Performance**: PWAs are known for their fast loading times and smooth interactions, giving users a responsive and engaging experience.
3. **Engagement**: PWAs can send push notifications, helping you re-engage users and keep them informed about updates or new content.
4. **Installability**: Users can "install" PWAs on their devices by adding them to the home screen or app menu, providing easy access without going through an app store.
5. **Safety**: PWAs are served over HTTPS, ensuring data security and privacy.

Key Technologies Behind PWAs

To build PWAs, you need to understand the core technologies that make them possible:

- **Service Workers**: These are JavaScript scripts that run in the background, intercepting network requests, and enabling features like offline caching and push notifications.

- **Web App Manifest**: A JSON file that provides metadata about the app, including its name, icons, and preferred display mode.

- **HTTPS**: PWAs must be served over HTTPS to ensure data security and trustworthiness.

Building Blocks of a PWA

Creating a PWA involves the following steps:

1. **Basic Setup**: Start with a web app that uses HTML, CSS, and JavaScript. Ensure your site is served over HTTPS.
2. **Service Worker**: Implement a service worker script to cache essential assets and enable offline functionality.
3. **Web App Manifest**: Create a web app manifest file to define your app's metadata and icons.
4. **Responsive Design**: Make your app responsive to ensure it looks and functions well on various devices and screen sizes.
5. **Offline Support**: Define caching strategies to allow your app to work offline or in low-network conditions.
6. **Push Notifications**: Implement push notifications to engage users and keep them informed.
7. **Installability**: Enable users to install your PWA on their devices for a more app-like experience.
8. **Testing and Debugging**: Test your PWA thoroughly, and use browser developer tools to debug any issues.
9. **Deployment**: Deploy your PWA to a web server or hosting platform.

10. **Monitoring and Analytics**: Implement monitoring and analytics to track user engagement and app performance.

In the upcoming sections of this chapter, we will delve deeper into each of these steps, providing practical examples and code snippets to guide you in building your Progressive Web App with TypeScript.

Section 14.2: Service Workers in TypeScript

Service workers are a fundamental part of building Progressive Web Apps (PWAs). They are JavaScript scripts that run in the background and enable advanced features such as caching, offline support, and push notifications. In this section, we'll explore how to work with service workers using TypeScript.

Setting Up a Service Worker

To get started with service workers in TypeScript, you'll need to create a TypeScript file for your service worker and configure your web application to use it. Here are the essential steps:

1. **Create a Service Worker TypeScript File**: Begin by creating a TypeScript file for your service worker, e.g., service-worker.ts.
2. **Register the Service Worker**: In your main application file (e.g., app.ts), register the service worker using the navigator.serviceWorker.register method.

```typescript
// app.ts

if ('serviceWorker' in navigator) {

navigator.serviceWorker.register('/service-worker.js')

.then((registration) => {
```

```
console.log('Service Worker registered with scope:',
registration.scope);
```

```
})
```

```
.catch((error) => {
```

```
console.error('Service Worker registration failed:', error);
```

```
});
```

```
}
```

1. **Service Worker Lifecycle**: Service workers have a lifecycle that includes installation, activation, and fetch events. You can add event listeners to handle these events.

```
// service-worker.ts
```

```
self.addEventListener('install', (event) => {
```

```
// Perform installation tasks, e.g., caching assets
```

```
});
```

```
self.addEventListener('activate', (event) => {
```

```
// Clean up old caches and activate the service worker
```

```
});
```

```
self.addEventListener('fetch', (event) => {
```

```
// Intercept network requests and respond with cached data if available
```

```
});
```

Caching Assets

One of the primary purposes of a service worker is to cache essential assets for offline use. You can use the Cache API in your service worker to achieve this. Here's an example of caching assets during the installation phase:

```typescript
// service-worker.ts

const cacheName = 'my-app-cache-v1';

const assetsToCache = [

'/',

'/index.html',

'/styles.css',

'/script.js',

'/images/logo.png',

];

self.addEventListener('install', (event) => {

event.waitUntil(

caches.open(cacheName)

.then((cache) => {

return cache.addAll(assetsToCache);

})

);
```

```
});
```

This code snippet opens a cache named my-app-cache-v1 and adds specified assets to it during service worker installation. You can then retrieve and serve these assets from the cache when the user is offline.

Offline Support

Service workers enable your PWA to work offline by intercepting network requests and responding with cached data. To achieve this, you can add a fetch event listener to your service worker, as shown earlier. When a network request is made, the service worker can check the cache for a matching response and return it if available.

```
// service-worker.ts

self.addEventListener('fetch', (event) => {

event.respondWith(

caches.match(event.request)

.then((response) => {

return response || fetch(event.request);

})

);

});
```

In this code, the service worker attempts to match the incoming network request with a cached response. If a match is found, it responds with the cached data; otherwise, it fetches the data from the network.

Updating the Service Worker

When you make changes to your service worker script, it's crucial to update the service worker to ensure that users receive the latest version of your app. You can achieve this by incrementing the cache name in your service worker and adding logic to activate the new service worker when it's ready.

```typescript
// service-worker.ts

const newCacheName = 'my-app-cache-v2';

self.addEventListener('install', (event) => {

// ...

// Activate the new service worker and clean up old caches

event.waitUntil(

caches.keys()

.then((cacheNames) => {

return Promise.all(

cacheNames.map((cache) => {

if (cache !== newCacheName) {

return caches.delete(cache);

}

})

);

})
```

```
);

});
```

This code snippet increments the cache name to my-app-cache-v2 and, during activation, deletes any old caches to ensure a smooth transition to the new service worker.

Conclusion

Service workers are a vital component of building Progressive Web Apps that offer offline capabilities and enhanced performance. In this section, we've explored the basics of working with service workers in TypeScript, including setting up, caching assets, providing offline support, and updating the service worker. By mastering service workers, you can create PWAs that provide a seamless user experience, even in challenging network conditions.

Section 14.3: Offline Support and Caching

Offline support is a critical feature of Progressive Web Apps (PWAs) that enhances user experience by allowing the application to function even when there is no internet connection. Caching plays a pivotal role in providing this functionality, as it enables the app to store and retrieve essential assets locally. In this section, we'll delve into offline support and caching strategies in TypeScript PWAs.

Caching Strategies

Caching in PWAs involves storing assets like HTML, CSS, JavaScript, and images on the user's device so that they can be accessed even without an internet connection. Various caching strategies can be employed based on the type of assets and the desired behavior. Here are some common caching strategies:

1. **Cache-First Strategy**: This strategy checks the cache for a response first. If the response is found in the cache, it's returned; otherwise, a network request is made. This strategy is suitable for assets that rarely change, like images.
2. **Network-First Strategy**: In this strategy, a network request is attempted first. If the network request is successful, the response is returned. If there's a network error, the response is retrieved from the cache. This is suitable for assets that frequently change, like news articles.
3. **Cache-Only Strategy**: This strategy attempts to fetch the response from the cache and doesn't make a network request. It's useful for ensuring that certain assets are always available offline.

Implementing Caching in Service Workers

Service workers are responsible for managing caching in PWAs. Here's a basic example of implementing caching using a service worker:

// service-worker.ts

```typescript
const CACHE_NAME = 'my-app-cache-v1';

const urlsToCache = [

'/',

'/index.html',

'/styles.css',

'/script.js',

'/images/logo.png',
```

```javascript
];

self.addEventListener('install', (event) => {

event.waitUntil(

caches.open(CACHE_NAME)

.then((cache) => {

return cache.addAll(urlsToCache);

})

);

});

self.addEventListener('fetch', (event) => {

event.respondWith(

caches.match(event.request)

.then((response) => {

return response || fetch(event.request);

})

);

});
```

In this example, we create a cache named my-app-cache-v1 during service worker installation and add specified URLs to it. When a fetch event occurs, the service worker attempts to match the request with a cached response. If a match is found, the cached response is returned; otherwise, a network request is made.

Cache Versioning and Updating

To ensure that users receive the latest version of your app, it's essential to implement cache versioning. When you make changes to your app's assets or service worker script, you can increment the cache version, prompting the service worker to update the cache accordingly. This prevents users from being stuck with outdated assets.

Dynamic Caching

Dynamic caching involves caching assets based on user interactions or application logic. For instance, you might cache data retrieved from an API in response to user actions. This enhances offline capabilities by allowing the app to serve data that was fetched when the user was online.

```typescript
// service-worker.ts

self.addEventListener('fetch', (event) => {

if (event.request.url.startsWith('https://api.example.com')) {

// Cache data from API responses

event.respondWith(

caches.open('api-data-cache')

.then((cache) => {

return cache.match(event.request)

.then((response) => {

return response || fetch(event.request)
```

```
.then((networkResponse) => {

cache.put(event.request, networkResponse.clone());

return networkResponse;

});

});

})

);

}

});
```

Conclusion

Offline support and caching are vital aspects of building PWAs that provide a seamless user experience. By implementing caching strategies in your TypeScript PWAs, you can ensure that your application remains accessible and performs well, even when users are offline or on slow networks. Caching not only improves reliability but also reduces data usage and speeds up load times, making your PWA a valuable tool for users in various conditions.

Section 14.4: Installable PWAs

Progressive Web Apps (PWAs) have the unique capability of being installed on a user's device, providing an app-like experience. This section explores the concept of making your TypeScript-based PWA installable, allowing users to add your web app to their home screens or app drawers.

The Web App Manifest

The first step in making your PWA installable is to create a **Web App Manifest**. This is a JSON file (usually named manifest.json) that provides metadata about your web app. It includes details like the app's name, icons, colors, and the URL where the app can be accessed.

Here's a basic example of a manifest.json file:

```
{

"name": "My PWA",

"short_name": "PWA",

"description": "A sample Progressive Web App",

"start_url": "/",

"display": "standalone",

"background_color": "#ffffff",

"theme_color": "#000000",

"icons": [

{

"src": "/icons/icon-192x192.png",

"sizes": "192x192",

"type": "image/png"

}

]
```

}

- name and short_name: The full and short names of your app, respectively.

- description: A brief description of your app.

- start_url: The URL where your app should start when launched.

- display: Specifies how the app should be displayed. "standalone" makes it feel like a native app.

- background_color and theme_color: Define the app's background and theme colors.

- icons: An array of icon objects with different sizes for various devices.

Adding the Manifest to Your HTML

To make your PWA aware of the Web App Manifest, you need to include a reference to it in the HTML of your app. Add the following code within the <head> element of your HTML:

<link rel="manifest" href="/manifest.json">

This tells the browser where to find the manifest file.

Prompting the User to Install

Once your PWA has a manifest, you can prompt users to install it when certain conditions are met. The most common way to do this is to use the beforeinstallprompt event.

// main.js

```typescript
let deferredPrompt;

window.addEventListener('beforeinstallprompt', (e) => {

e.preventDefault();

deferredPrompt = e;

// Display an "Install" button or similar UI element

installButton.style.display = 'block';

});

installButton.addEventListener('click', () => {

if (deferredPrompt) {

deferredPrompt.prompt();

deferredPrompt.userChoice.then((choiceResult) => {

if (choiceResult.outcome === 'accepted') {

console.log('User accepted the PWA installation');

} else {

console.log('User dismissed the PWA installation');

}

deferredPrompt = null;

});

}

});
```

In this code, we listen for the beforeinstallprompt event, which fires when the browser determines that your PWA is eligible for installation. We prevent the default behavior and store the event in deferredPrompt. You can then display an "Install" button or UI element and, when clicked, call prompt() on the deferredPrompt to trigger the installation prompt.

Service Worker Update for Installation

When a user installs your PWA, it's a good practice to update your service worker to cache the necessary assets and enable offline functionality. You can do this during the installation process or when the app is launched for the first time.

```javascript
// service-worker.js

self.addEventListener('install', (event) => {

// Cache assets during installation

event.waitUntil(

caches.open('my-app-cache-v2').then((cache) => {

return cache.addAll([

'/',

'/index.html',

'/styles.css',

// Add more URLs to cache as needed

]);

})
```

```
);

});
```

Remember to increment the cache version (e.g., my-app-cache-v2) whenever you make significant changes to your app's assets or service worker.

Conclusion

By creating a Web App Manifest, adding a reference to it in your HTML, and using the beforeinstallprompt event, you can make your TypeScript-based PWA installable on users' devices. Providing a seamless installation experience can help increase user engagement and retention, as PWAs are accessible right from the home screen, eliminating the need to navigate through browsers. Additionally, ensuring your service worker caches the necessary assets during installation enhances offline functionality, making your PWA even more valuable to users.

Section 14.5: Testing and Optimizing PWAs

Testing and optimizing Progressive Web Apps (PWAs) is crucial to ensure that they deliver the best possible user experience across different devices and network conditions. This section covers the key aspects of testing and optimizing PWAs built using TypeScript.

1. Performance Testing

Performance is a critical factor for PWAs. You can use tools like Google Lighthouse, WebPageTest, or Google PageSpeed Insights to analyze your PWA's performance. These tools provide valuable insights into areas where your PWA can be optimized for faster loading and responsiveness.

2. Responsiveness

PWAs should be responsive and work seamlessly on various screen sizes and orientations. Test your PWA on different devices and use browser developer tools to emulate different screen sizes and orientations. Ensure that your app adapts well to these changes.

3. Offline Testing

Test your PWA's offline capabilities thoroughly. You can do this by disabling network access in your browser's developer tools and checking if your app still functions correctly. Ensure that the service worker caches essential assets and that the app provides a meaningful offline experience.

4. Cross-Browser Compatibility

PWAs should work consistently across different browsers. Test your PWA on various browsers such as Chrome, Firefox, Safari, and Edge. Address any browser-specific issues to ensure a broad user reach.

5. Accessibility

Accessibility is critical for ensuring that your PWA is usable by all users, including those with disabilities. Use accessibility testing tools like Axe or the built-in browser accessibility audits to identify and fix accessibility issues.

6. Security Testing

Security is paramount for web applications. Test your PWA for common security vulnerabilities such as Cross-Site Scripting (XSS) and Cross-Site Request Forgery (CSRF). Ensure that your PWA follows secure coding practices.

7. Load Testing

Perform load testing to assess how your PWA handles a high volume of concurrent users. Tools like Apache JMeter or Gatling can help simulate heavy traffic and identify performance bottlenecks.

8. Optimization Techniques

Optimize your PWA for faster loading and improved user experience:

- Minimize and compress JavaScript, CSS, and image files.

- Use lazy loading for images and resources that are not immediately needed.

- Implement code splitting to load only the necessary code for each page.

- Optimize images for the web by reducing their size and using modern formats like WebP.

- Utilize browser caching to reduce load times for returning users.

9. User Testing

Conduct user testing with real users to gather feedback and identify usability issues. This can help you make user-centric improvements to your PWA.

10. Progressive Enhancement

Follow the principle of progressive enhancement by ensuring that your PWA functions even in browsers that do not support all PWA features. This approach ensures a wider user base.

11. Continuous Monitoring

After launching your PWA, continuously monitor its performance, security, and user feedback. Implement error tracking and monitoring solutions to proactively identify and resolve issues.

In conclusion, testing and optimizing your TypeScript-based PWA are ongoing processes that require attention to performance, responsiveness, accessibility, security, and user experience. Regularly assess your PWA using testing tools, real user feedback, and optimization techniques to ensure that it delivers a high-quality experience to all users, regardless of their devices and network conditions.

Chapter 15: Deploying TypeScript Applications

Section 15.1: Deployment Strategies

Deploying TypeScript applications is a crucial step in the software development lifecycle. It involves making your application accessible to users, whether they are accessing it from a web browser or another client. In this section, we will explore various deployment strategies and best practices for deploying TypeScript applications.

15.1.1 Overview of Deployment

Deployment is the process of making your TypeScript application available for use. This can involve various components and configurations, depending on the type of application you're deploying. Common deployment targets for TypeScript applications include web servers, cloud platforms, and containerized environments.

15.1.2 Deployment Targets

15.1.2.1 Web Servers

Deploying a TypeScript web application to a web server is one of the most common deployment scenarios. In this setup, you typically deploy your application to a web server like Apache, Nginx, or Microsoft IIS. These web servers are responsible for handling incoming HTTP requests and serving your application's content.

15.1.2.2 Cloud Platforms

Cloud platforms such as AWS (Amazon Web Services), Azure, Google Cloud, and Heroku provide infrastructure for deploying TypeScript applications. These platforms offer services like virtual machines, container orchestration, and serverless computing, allowing you to scale your application easily.

15.1.2.3 Containerized Environments

Containerization with technologies like Docker has gained popularity for deploying TypeScript applications. Containers encapsulate your application and its dependencies, making it easy to maintain consistency across different environments.

15.1.3 Deployment Process

15.1.3.1 Build and Compilation

Before deploying your TypeScript application, you need to build and compile it. TypeScript code is typically transpiled to JavaScript, and assets like CSS and images are optimized and bundled.

15.1.3.2 Configuration Management

Configuration management is crucial for deployment. You may need different configurations for development, staging, and production environments. Environment variables and configuration files are commonly used for this purpose.

15.1.3.3 Continuous Integration and Continuous Deployment (CI/CD)

Implementing CI/CD pipelines automates the deployment process. CI/CD tools like Jenkins, Travis CI, CircleCI, and GitHub Actions help ensure that changes are tested and deployed consistently.

15.1.3.4 Version Control

Using version control systems like Git allows you to track changes and easily roll back to previous versions in case of issues during deployment.

15.1.4 Deployment Strategies

15.1.4.1 Blue-Green Deployment

Blue-green deployment involves having two separate environments: the "blue" environment (the current live version) and the "green" environment (the new version). Traffic is gradually switched from blue to green, allowing for easy rollbacks if issues arise.

15.1.4.2 Canary Deployment

Canary deployment releases new features or updates to a small subset of users before rolling them out to the entire user base. This strategy helps identify potential issues early.

15.1.4.3 Rollback and Rollforward

Having rollback and rollforward mechanisms in place is essential. Rollback allows you to revert to a previous version in case of problems, while rollforward lets you move forward with a new version when issues are resolved.

15.1.5 Monitoring and Error Tracking

Monitoring your deployed application is crucial for detecting performance issues and errors. Tools like Prometheus, Grafana, Sentry, and New Relic provide insights into your application's health and performance in production.

15.1.6 Security Considerations

Security is paramount during deployment. Ensure that you follow security best practices, such as setting up firewalls, securing API endpoints, and regularly applying security patches.

15.1.7 Scalability

Consider the scalability of your deployment. Cloud platforms offer auto-scaling capabilities, allowing your application to handle increased traffic without manual intervention.

15.1.8 Conclusion

Deploying TypeScript applications involves multiple considerations, from choosing deployment targets to implementing deployment strategies and ensuring security and scalability. A well-planned deployment process is essential for delivering a reliable and performant application to your users.

Section 15.2: Hosting and Server Configuration

Hosting and server configuration are fundamental aspects of deploying TypeScript applications. Once you've built and prepared your application for deployment, you need to choose a hosting environment and configure your server settings to ensure your application runs smoothly. In this section, we'll delve into hosting options and essential server configurations for deploying TypeScript applications.

15.2.1 Hosting Options

15.2.1.1 Shared Hosting

Shared hosting is suitable for small to medium-sized websites and applications. It involves sharing server resources with other users on the same server. Providers like Bluehost and SiteGround offer shared hosting plans with varying levels of resources and features.

15.2.1.2 Virtual Private Server (VPS)

A Virtual Private Server (VPS) provides more control and dedicated resources compared to shared hosting. It's a cost-effective option for hosting TypeScript applications. Providers like DigitalOcean, Linode, and AWS Lightsail offer VPS hosting with customizable configurations.

15.2.1.3 Dedicated Server

Dedicated server hosting provides an entire physical server dedicated to your application. This option is suitable for large-scale applications with high resource demands. Providers like Liquid Web and OVH offer dedicated server hosting.

15.2.1.4 Cloud Hosting

Cloud hosting platforms such as AWS, Azure, Google Cloud, and DigitalOcean offer scalable and flexible hosting solutions. You can deploy TypeScript applications on virtual machines, container clusters, or serverless environments.

15.2.2 Server Configuration

15.2.2.1 Web Server Software

Choosing the right web server software is crucial. Common options include:

- **Nginx:** Known for its performance and reverse proxy capabilities.

- **Apache:** A versatile and widely used web server.

- **Caddy:** An easy-to-configure web server with automatic HTTPS.

- **IIS (Internet Information Services):** Microsoft's web server for Windows environments.

15.2.2.2 SSL/TLS Configuration

Enabling SSL/TLS encryption is essential to secure data transmitted between the client and server. You can obtain SSL certificates from providers like Let's Encrypt or commercial certificate authorities.

15.2.2.3 Domain Configuration

Set up domain names and configure DNS records to point to your server's IP address. Domain registrars like Namecheap and GoDaddy offer domain management services.

15.2.2.4 Firewall and Security

Implement a firewall to control incoming and outgoing traffic. Configure security settings to protect your server from common threats like DDoS attacks and brute force login attempts.

15.2.2.5 Content Delivery Network (CDN)

Consider using a CDN like Cloudflare or Akamai to cache and deliver static assets closer to users, reducing latency and improving load times.

15.2.3 Deployment Tools

Utilize deployment tools and automation scripts to streamline the deployment process. Tools like Ansible, Chef, and Puppet help manage server configurations and software installations.

15.2.4 Server Maintenance

Regularly update server software, apply security patches, and perform backups to ensure the stability and security of your deployed TypeScript application.

15.2.5 Load Balancing

For high-traffic applications, load balancing distributes incoming requests across multiple servers to improve performance and redundancy.

15.2.6 Serverless Deployment

Consider serverless architectures using platforms like AWS Lambda, Azure Functions, or Google Cloud Functions for event-driven and microservices-based applications.

15.2.7 Conclusion

Hosting and server configuration are pivotal aspects of deploying TypeScript applications successfully. The choice of hosting environment, server software, security measures, and automation tools significantly impacts the performance, scalability, and reliability of your application in a production environment. Careful planning and ongoing maintenance are key to ensuring your application runs smoothly and securely.

Section 15.3: Dockerizing TypeScript Apps

Docker has become a popular choice for containerizing and deploying applications. In this section, we'll explore how to Dockerize your TypeScript application, making it portable and consistent across different environments.

15.3.1 What is Docker?

Docker is a platform for developing, shipping, and running applications inside containers. Containers are lightweight, standalone, and executable packages that contain everything needed to run a piece of software, including the code, runtime, system tools, and libraries. Docker provides a consistent environment, ensuring that your application behaves the same way on a developer's machine, a testing server, or a production server.

15.3.2 Dockerizing a TypeScript Application

To Dockerize a TypeScript application, you'll need to create a Dockerfile, which is a configuration file that defines how your application should be packaged into a container. Here's a basic example of a Dockerfile for a TypeScript app:

```
# Use an official Node.js runtime as a parent image

FROM node:14

# Set the working directory in the container

WORKDIR /usr/src/app

# Copy package.json and package-lock.json to the container

COPY package*.json ./

# Install application dependencies

RUN npm install

# Copy the rest of the application source code to the container

COPY . .

# Build the TypeScript application

RUN npm run build

# Expose a port for the application

EXPOSE 8080
```

 # Define the command to run your application

CMD ["node", "dist/index.js"]

In this Dockerfile:

- We start with an official Node.js image as our base image.

- We set the working directory in the container to /usr/src/app.

- We copy package.json and package-lock.json to the container and install application dependencies.

- The source code is copied into the container.

- The TypeScript application is built using npm run build.

- We expose port 8080, which is the port our application will listen on.

- Finally, we specify the command to run our application.

15.3.3 Building a Docker Image

Once you have a Dockerfile, you can build a Docker image by running the following command in your project directory:

docker build -t my-typescript-app .

This command tells Docker to build an image named my-typescript-app using the Dockerfile in the current directory (.).

15.3.4 Running a Docker Container

To run a Docker container from the image you built, use the following command:

docker run -p 8080:8080 my-typescript-app

This command maps port 8080 from the container to port 8080 on your host machine. You can access your TypeScript application by navigating to http://localhost:8080 in your web browser.

15.3.5 Docker Compose

For more complex applications with multiple services, you can use Docker Compose to define and run multi-container Docker applications. Docker Compose uses a YAML file to configure the services, networks, and volumes for your application.

15.3.6 Benefits of Docker

Docker offers several advantages for deploying TypeScript applications:

- **Portability:** Docker containers can run consistently across different environments, reducing the "it works on my machine" problem.

- **Isolation:** Containers are isolated from each other, providing a high degree of security and preventing conflicts between dependencies.

- **Scalability:** Docker makes it easy to scale your application by running multiple containers in parallel.

- **Version Control:** Docker images can be versioned, ensuring that specific versions of your application can be deployed.

15.3.7 Conclusion

Dockerizing your TypeScript application streamlines the deployment process, making it easier to manage dependencies, ensure consistency across environments, and scale your application as needed. It's a valuable tool for modern software development and DevOps practices.

Section 15.4: Continuous Deployment with CI/CD

Continuous Integration and Continuous Deployment (CI/CD) is a crucial aspect of modern software development. In this section, we'll explore how to set up CI/CD pipelines for your TypeScript applications to automate the deployment process.

15.4.1 What is CI/CD?

CI/CD is a set of practices and tools that automate the building, testing, and deployment of code changes. It aims to deliver code to production more frequently and reliably. CI focuses on automating the integration of code changes into a shared repository, while CD automates the deployment of code changes to production or staging environments.

15.4.2 Setting Up CI/CD

To set up CI/CD for your TypeScript application, you'll need to choose a CI/CD platform or service. Popular choices include

Jenkins, Travis CI, CircleCI, GitLab CI/CD, and GitHub Actions. Here's a high-level overview of the CI/CD process:

1. **Code Repository**: Ensure your TypeScript application's code is hosted in a version control system (e.g., Git) in a repository.
2. **CI Configuration**: Create a configuration file (e.g., .travis.yml for Travis CI) that defines the build and test steps for your application. This file typically includes instructions for installing dependencies, building the application, and running tests.
3. **Integration**: Whenever changes are pushed to the repository, the CI server (e.g., Travis CI) automatically triggers the configured build and test process.
4. **Testing**: Automated tests, including unit tests and end-to-end tests, are executed to ensure the code changes are valid.
5. **Deployment**: If the tests pass successfully, the CI/CD pipeline can proceed with the deployment phase. This may involve packaging the application, creating Docker images, and deploying to staging or production servers.
6. **Monitoring**: Continuous monitoring and logging are essential to detect and diagnose issues in production.

15.4.3 Benefits of CI/CD

Implementing CI/CD for your TypeScript applications offers several advantages:

- **Faster Development**: CI/CD streamlines the development process by automating many tasks, reducing manual effort and errors.

- **Quality Assurance**: Automated testing ensures that code changes don't introduce regressions, helping maintain code quality.

- **Consistency**: CI/CD promotes consistency in the build and deployment process, reducing the risk of issues related to environment differences.

- **Quick Feedback**: Developers receive rapid feedback on the quality of their code changes, allowing them to address issues early.

- **Deployment Safety**: Automated deployments are typically safer and more reliable than manual deployments.

15.4.4 CI/CD Platforms

Here's a brief overview of some CI/CD platforms and their integration with TypeScript projects:

- **Travis CI**: Supports TypeScript projects and offers easy integration with GitHub repositories.

- **CircleCI**: Provides powerful customization options for building and deploying TypeScript applications.

- **GitLab CI/CD**: Offers built-in CI/CD capabilities and tight integration with GitLab repositories.

- **GitHub Actions**: Seamlessly integrates with GitHub repositories, making it convenient for TypeScript projects hosted on GitHub.

15.4.5 Example CI Configuration

Here's a simplified example of a .travis.yml file for a TypeScript project using Travis CI:

language: node_js

node_js:

- 14

install:

- npm install

script:

- npm test

deploy:

provider: heroku

api_key: $HEROKU_API_KEY

app: your-app-name

In this example, Travis CI sets up a Node.js environment, installs dependencies, runs tests, and deploys the application to Heroku when changes are pushed to the repository.

15.4.6 Conclusion

CI/CD is a critical part of modern software development practices, enabling faster development, higher code quality, and more reliable deployments. Setting up CI/CD pipelines for your TypeScript applications can greatly improve your development workflow and the overall quality of your software. Choose a CI/CD platform that best suits your project's needs and start automating your development and deployment processes today.

Section 15.5: Monitoring and Error Tracking

Monitoring and error tracking are essential components of maintaining a healthy production environment for your TypeScript applications. In this section, we'll explore why monitoring is crucial, tools you can use, and best practices for error tracking.

15.5.1 The Importance of Monitoring

Monitoring provides visibility into your application's performance and helps you identify and resolve issues before they impact users. Here are some key reasons why monitoring is essential:

- **Performance Optimization**: Monitoring allows you to identify bottlenecks and areas where your application can be optimized for better performance.

- **Proactive Issue Detection**: It helps you catch issues early, preventing potential outages or downtimes.

- **User Experience Improvement**: By monitoring user interactions, you can gain insights into how users are using your application and make improvements accordingly.

- **Security**: Monitoring can help you detect and respond to security incidents promptly.

15.5.2 Types of Monitoring

There are various types of monitoring you can implement for your TypeScript applications:

- **Application Performance Monitoring (APM)**: APM tools monitor the performance of your application in terms of response times, resource usage, and error rates.

- **Infrastructure Monitoring**: This type of monitoring focuses on the underlying infrastructure, such as server CPU and memory usage, network latency, and disk space.

- **User Monitoring**: User monitoring tracks user interactions with your application, including page views, clicks, and other actions.

- **Error Monitoring**: Error monitoring tools track and report errors and exceptions that occur in your application's code.

15.5.3 Monitoring Tools

Several monitoring tools and services are available for TypeScript applications:

- **Prometheus**: An open-source monitoring and alerting toolkit designed for reliability and scalability.

- **Grafana**: Often used in conjunction with Prometheus, Grafana provides visualization and dashboard capabilities for monitoring data.

- **New Relic**: Offers APM, infrastructure, and user monitoring for web applications.

- **Sentry**: A popular error tracking tool that helps you identify and diagnose issues in your code.

- **ELK Stack (Elasticsearch, Logstash, Kibana)**: Used for log and event data analysis, helpful for debugging and monitoring.

- **Datadog**: Provides a wide range of monitoring and observability solutions.

15.5.4 Error Tracking Best Practices

When it comes to error tracking, here are some best practices to consider:

- **Centralized Logging**: Implement centralized logging to collect and store log data from your TypeScript application. Tools like ELK Stack or cloud-based log management services can help.

- **Automated Alerts**: Set up automated alerts to be notified immediately when critical errors occur. This allows you to respond promptly and prevent extended downtime.

- **Error Grouping**: Group similar error occurrences together to avoid receiving separate notifications for the same issue. This makes it easier to prioritize and address problems.

- **Error Context**: Capture additional context when an error occurs, such as user information, request details, and environment variables. This information can be invaluable for debugging.

• **Version Tracking**: Track errors by application version to identify whether a particular issue is specific to a release.

15.5.5 TypeScript and Monitoring

TypeScript's static typing can help prevent certain types of errors before they occur, but runtime errors can still happen. Therefore, it's essential to include TypeScript error tracking in your monitoring strategy. Tools like Sentry offer TypeScript support, making it easier to track and resolve type-related errors in your application.

15.5.6 Conclusion

Monitoring and error tracking are critical for maintaining the reliability and performance of your TypeScript applications. By implementing the right monitoring tools and following best practices, you can proactively identify and address issues, ultimately providing a better experience for your users and ensuring the success of your applications in production.

Chapter 16: Scaling and Performance Optimization

In this chapter, we will delve into the critical aspects of scaling and performance optimization for TypeScript applications. As your application gains users and traffic, ensuring it remains performant becomes crucial. We will explore various techniques and strategies to optimize the performance of your TypeScript applications and handle increased loads.

Section 16.1: Performance Profiling and Analysis

Performance profiling and analysis are fundamental steps in identifying bottlenecks and areas for improvement in your TypeScript application. Profiling allows you to gather data about how your application performs, which can then be analyzed to pinpoint performance issues. Let's dive into the details of performance profiling and analysis.

16.1.1 Why Performance Profiling?

Performance profiling is essential for several reasons:

- **Identifying Bottlenecks**: Profiling helps you identify parts of your code that are causing performance bottlenecks, such as slow functions or excessive memory usage.

- **Optimization Prioritization**: It helps you prioritize optimizations based on data, focusing your efforts where they will have the most significant impact.

- **Regression Detection**: Profiling can be used to detect performance regressions when changes are made to your codebase.

16.1.2 Profiling Tools

There are various profiling tools available for TypeScript applications, each serving a specific purpose:

- **Chrome DevTools**: Chrome's developer tools provide built-in profiling capabilities for JavaScript and TypeScript. You can use the Performance and Memory tabs to record and analyze performance data.

- **Node.js Profiler**: For server-side TypeScript applications, Node.js includes built-in profilers that can be used to profile CPU and memory usage.

- **Webpack Bundle Analyzer**: If you're bundling your TypeScript code with Webpack, the Webpack Bundle Analyzer can help you visualize the size and contents of your bundles, optimizing bundle size.

- **Lighthouse**: Lighthouse is a Chrome extension for auditing web page performance and generating performance reports. It can help identify performance issues on the client side.

- **Jest Profiling**: If you're using Jest for testing your TypeScript code, it includes profiling capabilities to measure test suite performance.

16.1.3 Profiling Process

Here's a high-level process for performance profiling:

1. **Identify What to Profile**: Determine which parts of your application you want to profile. This could be a specific function, a route, or the entire application.
2. **Instrument Your Code**: Depending on the profiling tool, you may need to add instrumentation to your code to start and stop profiling sessions.
3. **Generate Profiling Data**: Run your application with profiling enabled, and gather performance data during the execution.
4. **Analyze the Data**: Use the profiling tool's interface to analyze the collected data. Look for CPU hotspots, memory leaks, or other performance issues.
5. **Optimize**: Once you've identified performance bottlenecks, work on optimizing those parts of your code. Make iterative improvements and reprofile to measure the impact.

16.1.4 Profiling in TypeScript

When profiling TypeScript applications, it's essential to understand that you'll be profiling the generated JavaScript code. Keep the following in mind:

- Profiling tools work with JavaScript, so you'll see JavaScript code in the reports, not TypeScript.

- Use source maps to map the JavaScript code back to your TypeScript source code, making it easier to locate performance bottlenecks in your TypeScript files.

In the upcoming sections of this chapter, we will explore various optimization techniques and strategies to improve the performance of your TypeScript applications based on the insights gained from profiling. Performance optimization is a continuous process that evolves with your application's growth, and it plays a crucial role in ensuring your application scales effectively.

Section 16.2: Code Splitting and Lazy Loading

Code splitting and lazy loading are optimization techniques that can significantly improve the performance of your TypeScript applications, especially in the context of single-page applications (SPAs) or large web applications. These techniques aim to reduce the initial bundle size and load only the necessary code when it's required. Let's explore code splitting and lazy loading in TypeScript applications.

16.2.1 Understanding Code Splitting

Code splitting is a technique that involves breaking your application's JavaScript bundle into smaller, more manageable chunks. Instead of loading the entire application code upfront, you load only the essential code needed for the initial page view. Additional code is loaded on-demand as the user interacts with the application.

Benefits of code splitting:

- **Faster Initial Load**: Smaller initial bundles lead to faster page load times, improving the user experience.

- **Reduced JavaScript Payload**: Code splitting reduces the size of the JavaScript payload sent to the client, which can lead to quicker downloads and parsing.

- **Optimized Caching**: Smaller bundles are more cacheable, benefiting returning users who have already loaded parts of the application.

16.2.2 Implementing Code Splitting

In TypeScript applications, code splitting can be implemented using module bundlers like Webpack or tools like dynamic import(). Here's how you can use Webpack for code splitting:

1. **Webpack Configuration**: In your Webpack configuration file, specify the optimization option for splitting chunks:

```js
// webpack.config.js

module.exports = {

// ...

optimization: {

splitChunks: {

chunks: 'all',

},

},

};
```

This configuration tells Webpack to split chunks for all modules, optimizing your bundles.

1. **Dynamic import()**: In your TypeScript code, you can use dynamic import() to load modules on-demand. For example:

```
const someModule = () => import('./someModule');
```

Webpack will create a separate chunk for someModule, and it will be loaded only when someModule is actually used.

16.2.3 Lazy Loading Routes

In the context of web applications with multiple routes, lazy loading routes is a common code splitting technique. It involves loading the code for each route only when the user navigates to that specific route. This approach can significantly reduce the initial bundle size.

For frameworks like Angular, React, or Vue.js, lazy loading routes is often a built-in feature. Here's a high-level overview of how you can implement lazy loading routes in a TypeScript-based React application:

1. **React Suspense and lazy()**: Use React's lazy() function to create a dynamic import for your route components. For example:

```
import { lazy, Suspense } from 'react';

const LazyComponent = lazy(() => import('./LazyComponent'));
```

```
const App = () => (

<Suspense fallback={<div>Loading...</div>}>

<LazyComponent />

</Suspense>

);
```

In this example, LazyComponent will be loaded on-demand when it's needed.

1. **Webpack Configuration**: Ensure your Webpack configuration is set up to support code splitting as described earlier.

By employing code splitting and lazy loading, you can significantly improve the initial load performance of your TypeScript applications, making them more responsive and efficient for users. These techniques are especially valuable when dealing with large and complex applications.

Section 16.3: Server-Side Rendering with TypeScript

Server-Side Rendering (SSR) is a technique that allows you to pre-render a web page on the server and send the fully-rendered HTML to the client. This approach can improve the performance and SEO (Search Engine Optimization) of your TypeScript applications. In this section, we'll explore SSR in the context of TypeScript.

16.3.1 Understanding Server-Side Rendering

The traditional approach to web development, known as Client-Side Rendering (CSR), involves loading a minimal HTML skeleton and using JavaScript to fetch and render the content. While CSR can provide a dynamic and interactive user experience, it can also result in slower initial page loads, which can negatively impact SEO and user engagement.

SSR, on the other hand, generates HTML on the server and sends it to the client, including the initial data. This means that when a user requests a page, they receive a fully-rendered HTML document, which can be beneficial for several reasons:

- **Improved Performance**: SSR reduces the time it takes for the initial page to load, as the client receives pre-rendered HTML.

- **Better SEO**: Search engines can easily crawl and index SSR pages since they receive fully-rendered HTML content.

- **Accessibility**: SSR pages often provide a better experience for users with disabilities or slower internet connections because they receive content faster.

16.3.2 Implementing SSR in TypeScript

To implement SSR in a TypeScript application, you can choose from various frameworks and libraries that support SSR, such as Next.js for React applications, Nuxt.js for Vue.js applications, or Angular Universal for Angular applications. Here's a high-level overview of implementing SSR with Next.js, a popular framework for React:

1. **Setup**: Install Next.js in your project and create a Next.js application.

npm install next react react-dom

1. **Page Components**: Create React components for the pages you want to render server-side. These components should be located in the pages directory.

// pages/index.tsx

```tsx
import React from 'react';

const HomePage: React.FC = () => {

return <div>Welcome to my SSR application!</div>;

};

export default HomePage;
```

1. **Server Configuration**: Next.js handles the server-side rendering for you. You can start the development server using the following command:

npx next dev

This command will start a development server that supports SSR.

1. **Build and Deploy**: When you're ready to deploy your SSR application, use the Next.js build command:

npx next build

You can then deploy the generated files to your hosting platform of choice.

Remember that SSR requires careful consideration of your application's state management, routing, and data fetching strategies, as some components and libraries designed for CSR may not work seamlessly with SSR.

By implementing Server-Side Rendering in your TypeScript applications, you can achieve improved performance and SEO, making your web applications more accessible and user-friendly. It's a valuable technique, especially for content-rich or e-commerce websites where SEO and initial load times are critical.

Section 16.4: Load Balancing and Scaling Techniques

Load balancing and scaling are essential techniques to ensure that your TypeScript web applications can handle a growing number of users and traffic without sacrificing performance or reliability. In this section, we'll explore load balancing and scaling strategies for TypeScript applications.

16.4.1 Understanding Load Balancing

Load balancing is the process of distributing incoming network traffic across multiple servers or resources to ensure that no single server becomes overloaded. Load balancers are typically placed in front of a group of servers, and they make decisions about how to distribute incoming requests based on factors like server health, capacity, and the specific algorithm configured.

Load balancing offers several benefits, including:

- **Improved Performance**: By distributing traffic evenly, load balancers prevent any single server from becoming a bottleneck, which can lead to faster response times for users.

- **High Availability**: Load balancers can detect when a server is unavailable or experiencing issues and redirect traffic to healthy servers, reducing downtime.

- **Scalability**: Load balancers can easily accommodate additional servers as your application scales, allowing you to handle more users and traffic.

16.4.2 Load Balancing Strategies

There are various load balancing strategies to consider when distributing incoming traffic:

- **Round Robin**: In this strategy, each incoming request is sent to the next server in the rotation. It's a simple and effective method for distributing traffic evenly.

- **Least Connections**: The load balancer routes requests to the server with the fewest active connections. This strategy is useful when server loads vary.

- **IP Hash**: Requests are directed to servers based on the client's IP address. This strategy can ensure that a specific client always connects to the same server.

- **Weighted Round Robin**: Servers are assigned different weights, and the load balancer takes these weights into account when distributing traffic. This is useful when some servers are more powerful than others.

- **Session Persistence**: Some applications require that a user's requests are consistently directed to the same server. Session persistence (also known as sticky sessions) ensures that requests from the same client go to the same server based on session information.

16.4.3 Scaling Techniques

Scaling involves adding more resources to your application infrastructure to handle increased load. There are two primary types of scaling:

- **Vertical Scaling (Scaling Up)**: In this approach, you increase the capacity of individual servers by adding more CPU, memory, or other resources. Vertical scaling can be limited by the maximum capacity of a single server and may involve downtime or service disruption during upgrades.

- **Horizontal Scaling (Scaling Out)**: Horizontal scaling involves adding more servers or instances to your application. This approach is more scalable and resilient than vertical scaling because it can accommodate a virtually unlimited number of users. It also allows for easy redundancy and fault tolerance.

16.4.4 TypeScript Application Scaling

To scale TypeScript applications, you can take advantage of cloud-based infrastructure services like Amazon Web Services (AWS), Microsoft Azure, or Google Cloud Platform (GCP). These platforms offer auto-scaling capabilities that can automatically add or remove instances based on demand.

Containerization and orchestration tools like Docker and Kubernetes also play a crucial role in managing and scaling TypeScript applications. You can containerize your application components and use Kubernetes to automate deployment, scaling, and load balancing.

Remember that scaling also involves optimizing your application's architecture, database, and caching strategies. Load testing and performance monitoring are essential to identify bottlenecks and ensure that your application scales effectively.

By implementing load balancing and scaling techniques, you can build highly available and performant TypeScript applications that can handle traffic spikes and growing user bases, providing a seamless experience to your users.

Section 16.5: Content Delivery Networks (CDNs)

Content Delivery Networks (CDNs) are a critical component of modern web applications that help improve performance, availability, and global reach. In this section, we'll explore CDNs and how they can benefit your TypeScript applications.

16.5.1 What is a CDN?

A CDN is a network of geographically distributed servers strategically placed at various locations worldwide. These servers store cached copies of your web application's static assets, such as images, stylesheets, JavaScript files, and even entire web pages. When a user requests content from your application, the CDN serves it from the server closest to the user, reducing latency and improving load times.

16.5.2 Key Benefits of Using CDNs

CDNs offer several advantages for TypeScript applications:

- **Improved Performance**: CDNs reduce latency by serving content from servers geographically closer to users. Faster load times lead to a better user experience.

- **Global Availability**: CDNs have servers in multiple regions, ensuring that your content is available and responsive to users worldwide.

- **Traffic Offloading**: CDNs handle the delivery of static assets, reducing the load on your application servers. This allows your servers to focus on dynamic content generation.

- **Load Balancing**: CDNs can distribute traffic across multiple servers, ensuring even distribution and high availability.

- **Distributed Caching**: CDNs cache static assets at various locations, reducing the need for repeated requests to your origin server and saving bandwidth.

- **DDoS Mitigation**: CDNs can absorb and mitigate Distributed Denial of Service (DDoS) attacks, protecting your application from downtime and service interruptions.

16.5.3 Implementing a CDN

To implement a CDN for your TypeScript application, follow these steps:

1. **Choose a CDN Provider**: Select a CDN provider that suits your needs. Popular CDN providers include Cloudflare, Akamai, Amazon CloudFront, and Microsoft Azure CDN.

2. **Create a CDN Distribution**: Set up a CDN distribution within your chosen CDN provider's dashboard. This involves configuring settings such as origin server, caching rules, and security options.

3. **Configure Your Application**: Update your application's static asset URLs to point to the CDN's domain. This typically involves changing URLs for images, stylesheets, scripts, and other assets.

4. **Set Caching Rules**: Configure caching rules on the CDN to determine how long assets should be cached. You can specify caching behavior based on file types, cache duration, and cache purging strategies.

5. **Security Configuration**: Enable security features provided by the CDN, such as SSL/TLS encryption, web application firewall (WAF), and DDoS protection.

6. **Testing and Monitoring**: Thoroughly test your application with the CDN in place to ensure that content is delivered correctly and that performance is improved. Set up monitoring to track CDN performance and troubleshoot any issues.

16.5.4 Cache Invalidation and Purging

One challenge when using CDNs is cache invalidation. Cached content may become outdated, and you need mechanisms to ensure that users always receive the latest versions of your assets. CDNs provide cache invalidation and purging options, allowing you to manually or programmatically remove cached content.

16.5.5 Cost Considerations

While CDNs offer significant benefits, they may come with associated costs. Pricing structures can vary, including pay-as-you-go models, subscription plans, and data transfer fees. Consider your application's traffic patterns and geographic distribution when evaluating CDN costs.

In conclusion, Content Delivery Networks are a valuable addition to TypeScript applications, enhancing performance, global availability, and security. By implementing a CDN, you can ensure that your application delivers a seamless experience to users around the world, even during traffic spikes and DDoS attacks.

Chapter 17: Accessibility and Internationalization

In Chapter 17, we will explore two essential aspects of web development: Accessibility and Internationalization (i18n). These topics are crucial for creating inclusive and user-friendly web applications that can reach a global audience. In this section, we'll focus on Accessibility.

Section 17.1: Building Accessible Web Applications

What is Web Accessibility?

Web accessibility, often abbreviated as "a11y" (a-11 characters between 'a' and 'y'), refers to the practice of making websites and web applications usable by people with disabilities. Disabilities can manifest in various forms, including visual, auditory, motor, or cognitive impairments. Web accessibility ensures that everyone, regardless of their abilities or disabilities, can perceive, understand, navigate, and interact with web content effectively.

The Importance of Web Accessibility

Web accessibility is not just a legal requirement in many regions; it's also a moral and ethical responsibility. Here are some key reasons why web accessibility is crucial:

- **Inclusivity**: Accessible websites include all users, broadening your audience and making your content available to a more diverse set of people.

- **Legal Compliance**: Many countries and regions have laws and regulations that mandate web accessibility. Non-compliance can lead to legal repercussions.

- **Better User Experience**: Improved accessibility often leads to a better user experience for all users, not just those with disabilities.

- **Search Engine Optimization (SEO)**: Accessible websites tend to have better SEO, as search engines can more easily understand and index the content.

Building Accessible Web Applications

Building accessible web applications involves several key principles and practices:

1. **Semantic HTML**: Use semantic HTML elements (e.g., <button>, <input>, <a>) correctly to provide meaningful structure and context to your content.
2. **Keyboard Navigation**: Ensure that all interactive elements can be operated and navigated using a keyboard alone. Test your application's keyboard accessibility thoroughly.
3. **Aria Roles and Attributes**: Use ARIA (Accessible Rich Internet Applications) roles and attributes to enhance the accessibility of complex widgets and dynamic content.
4. **Color Contrast**: Ensure sufficient color contrast between text and background to make content readable for users with visual impairments.
5. **Alternative Text**: Provide descriptive alt text for images and other non-text content to convey their meaning to screen readers.
6. **Focus Management**: Ensure that keyboard focus is visible

and logical, and that users can easily understand where they are in your application.

7. **Testing and Validation**: Regularly test your application with assistive technologies, such as screen readers, and use accessibility validation tools to identify and fix issues.

8. **Documentation**: Document your accessibility practices and guidelines to ensure that all team members are aware of and adhere to them.

By following these practices, you can make your web applications more inclusive and accessible to a wider audience.

In the next section, we'll dive into TypeScript-specific considerations for web accessibility and explore how TypeScript can be leveraged to create accessible user interfaces.

Section 17.2: TypeScript and Accessibility

In this section, we'll delve into how TypeScript, as a statically typed superset of JavaScript, can be used to enhance web accessibility. TypeScript provides tools and features that enable developers to write more robust and accessible code, making it easier to catch accessibility issues during development.

TypeScript's Type System for Accessibility

One of the primary benefits of TypeScript is its static type system. By explicitly defining types for variables, functions, and objects, TypeScript helps catch type-related errors at compile-time, reducing the likelihood of runtime issues. This type system can also be leveraged to improve accessibility.

Custom Type Definitions

To enhance accessibility, you can create custom type definitions that reflect the specific structure and properties of your application's accessible components. For example, you can define types for accessible buttons, forms, or navigation menus, ensuring that these components adhere to accessibility standards.

```typescript
// Custom type for an accessible button

type AccessibleButtonProps = {

label: string;

onClick: () => void;

disabled?: boolean;

// ... other accessibility-related properties

};

function AccessibleButton(props: AccessibleButtonProps) {

// Implementation of an accessible button

// Ensure that the button's attributes and behavior align with accessibility guidelines.

}
```

By using custom type definitions, you make it clear which properties are required for an accessible component and which are optional. This helps in maintaining consistent accessibility across your application.

Static Analysis and Linting

TypeScript integrates seamlessly with popular linting tools like ESLint and TSLint. You can extend these tools with accessibility-specific rules and plugins to catch accessibility violations early in the development process. For instance, you can enforce rules that check for missing alt attributes on images or require focus management in interactive elements.

// An ESLint rule for enforcing alt text on images

```
{

"rules": {

"jsx-a11y/alt-text": ["error", {

"elements": ["img"],

"img:altHasRole": ["Image"],

}],

},

}
```

By using static analysis and linting, you can maintain a consistent level of accessibility throughout your codebase and ensure that accessibility best practices are followed.

TypeScript and UI Frameworks

If you're building your web application using popular UI frameworks like React, Angular, or Vue.js, TypeScript can provide enhanced accessibility support. These frameworks often have type definitions that include accessibility-related information.

For example, React provides @types/react with types for HTML elements and ARIA attributes. This means that when you use these types in your TypeScript code, you get autocomplete suggestions and type checking for accessibility properties.

```
import React from 'react';

function MyComponent() {

return (

<button

onClick={() => {}}

aria-label="Close"

disabled={false}

>

X

</button>

);

}
```

By leveraging TypeScript's type system in combination with the type definitions provided by UI frameworks, you can create more accessible components with confidence.

In this section, we've explored how TypeScript's type system and static analysis capabilities can be used to enhance web accessibility. By creating custom type definitions, using static analysis and linting, and integrating TypeScript with UI frameworks, you can make significant strides in improving the accessibility of your web applications. In the next section, we'll shift our focus to internationalization (i18n) and how TypeScript can facilitate the localization of your web content.

Section 17.3: Internationalization (i18n) with TypeScript

In this section, we'll explore how TypeScript can be used to implement internationalization (i18n) in web applications. Internationalization is the process of designing and adapting your application to support multiple languages and regions. TypeScript's static typing and strong tooling support can greatly assist in creating maintainable and error-free i18n solutions.

Key Concepts of Internationalization

Before diving into TypeScript-specific techniques, let's review some essential concepts related to i18n:

1. Localization (L10n):

Localization involves adapting your application for a specific region or locale. It includes translating text, formatting numbers, dates, and currencies according to the target locale's conventions.

2. Internationalization (i18n):

Internationalization refers to the broader process of making your application capable of supporting multiple languages and regions. It encompasses not only localization but also the design and architecture of your application to handle different languages gracefully.

3. Message Catalogs:

Message catalogs are collections of localized text strings used in your application. Each language/locale has its message catalog, containing translations of the same text keys.

Using TypeScript for Internationalization

TypeScript's type safety and tooling can be valuable when working with i18n. Here's how TypeScript can be utilized for various aspects of internationalization:

1. String Typing:

TypeScript allows you to create custom types for strings used in your application. By defining type-safe strings, you can ensure that only valid keys from your message catalogs are used.

```typescript
// Custom type for localized strings

type LocalizedString = 'welcomeMessage' | 'goodbyeMessage';

// Usage

const welcome: LocalizedString = 'welcomeMessage';

const localizedString: string = getMessage(welcome);
```

2. Message Catalogs:

TypeScript can help maintain your message catalogs by ensuring that all required keys and translations are present. You can use code generation tools to generate TypeScript interfaces from your message catalogs.

```typescript
// Message catalog interface

interface MessageCatalog {

welcomeMessage: string;

goodbyeMessage: string;

}

// Usage

const messages: MessageCatalog = {

welcomeMessage: 'Welcome!',

goodbyeMessage: 'Goodbye!',

};
```

3. Pluralization and Formatting:

TypeScript can be used to create functions that handle pluralization and formatting according to the target locale's rules.

```typescript
// Pluralization function

function getPluralizedMessage(count: number, locale: string): string {

// Implement pluralization logic based on the locale

// Return the appropriate message

}

// Usage
```

```
const count = 3;
```

```
const message = getPluralizedMessage(count, 'en-US');
```

4. Tooling and IDE Support:

TypeScript-aware code editors, such as Visual Studio Code, provide autocompletion and type checking for localized strings and message catalogs. This helps catch localization-related errors early in the development process.

5. Libraries and Frameworks:

Many popular libraries and frameworks for i18n, such as i18next or react-intl, have TypeScript support. You can take advantage of TypeScript's type inference when using these libraries.

In conclusion, TypeScript can significantly improve the internationalization process of your web applications. By leveraging its strong typing, tooling, and code generation capabilities, you can create more robust and maintainable i18n solutions. In the next section, we'll delve into specific localization strategies and best practices to ensure that your application is not only multilingual but also culturally sensitive.

Section 17.4: Localization Strategies

In this section, we'll explore various strategies and best practices for implementing localization (L10n) in TypeScript-based web applications. Localization is the process of adapting your application for a specific region or locale, including translating text, formatting dates, numbers, and currencies according to local conventions.

1. Message Formatting and Pluralization

When localizing text, consider differences in sentence structure, word order, and grammar across languages. Use placeholder variables for dynamic content within messages and format them accordingly.

```
// English message

const englishMessage = 'Hello, {name}!';

// Spanish translation with reordered variables

const spanishTranslation = '¡Hola, {name}!';
```

Implement pluralization rules for quantities. Some languages have complex pluralization rules, so it's essential to handle singular, plural, and other grammatical forms.

```
// Pluralization function

function getPluralizedMessage(count: number, locale: string): string {

// Implement pluralization logic based on the locale

// Return the appropriate message

}

const count = 3;

const message = getPluralizedMessage(count, 'en-US');
```

2. Message Catalogs

Maintain separate message catalogs for each target language or locale. Each catalog should include translations for all text strings used in your application.

```typescript
// English message catalog

const englishMessages = {

greeting: 'Hello!',

goodbye: 'Goodbye!',

};

// Spanish message catalog

const spanishMessages = {

greeting: '¡Hola!',

goodbye: '¡Adiós!',

};
```

3. Date and Number Formatting

Ensure that dates, numbers, and currencies are formatted correctly for each locale. TypeScript provides the Intl object, which can format dates, numbers, and currencies based on the user's locale.

```typescript
const date = new Date();

const formattedDate = date.toLocaleDateString('fr-FR');

const formattedNumber = new Intl.NumberFormat('de-DE').format(12345.67);
```

4. Language Detection

Detect the user's preferred language or locale and use it to load the appropriate message catalog and apply formatting.

```
function getUserLocale(): string {

// Implement logic to detect user's preferred locale

// e.g., from browser settings or user preferences

}

const userLocale = getUserLocale();

const messages = loadMessagesForLocale(userLocale);
```

5. Translation Tools

Use translation management tools that support collaboration among translators and developers. These tools can help manage message catalogs, track changes, and streamline the localization workflow.

6. Testing and Validation

Thoroughly test your localized application to ensure that text fits within UI components, and there are no layout issues. Additionally, validate that all messages are correctly translated and formatted in each supported language.

7. Context-Aware Localization

Consider context when translating text. Some words or phrases may have multiple meanings, so providing context helps translators choose the appropriate translation.

```
// Provide context for translation

const messages = {

menu: {
```

```
file: {

label: 'File',

tooltip: 'Open a file',

},

},

};
```

8. Continuous Localization

Implement continuous localization practices to keep translations up-to-date as your application evolves. Automate the extraction of translatable strings from the codebase and integrate them into your localization workflow.

9. Cultural Sensitivity

Be culturally sensitive in your translations. Understand cultural norms, customs, and taboos to avoid unintentional offense in different regions.

10. Documentation

Document your localization process, including guidelines for translators, placeholders, and pluralization rules. Clear documentation ensures consistency in translations.

By following these localization strategies and best practices, you can create a more inclusive and accessible application that caters to users from various linguistic and cultural backgrounds. Effective localization enhances user experience and broadens your application's global reach.

Section 17.5: Testing for Accessibility and i18n

Testing for accessibility (A11y) and internationalization (i18n) is crucial to ensure that your web application is usable by people with disabilities and across different languages and cultures. In this section, we'll discuss strategies for testing these aspects in your TypeScript-based applications.

1. Accessibility Testing

Accessibility testing aims to identify and address issues that can hinder users with disabilities from using your application effectively. Here are some key considerations:

- **Screen Reader Testing:** Use screen reader software (e.g., VoiceOver, JAWS) to navigate your application and ensure it provides meaningful information and interactions.

- **Keyboard Navigation:** Test if all interactive elements and focusable components are accessible and usable using only a keyboard.

- **Semantic HTML:** Ensure you use semantic HTML elements (e.g., headings, buttons) correctly to provide meaningful structure and navigation.

- **ARIA Roles and Attributes:** Use ARIA (Accessible Rich Internet Applications) roles and attributes to enhance the accessibility of custom components and dynamic content.

- **Contrast Ratio:** Check that text and background colors have sufficient contrast for readability.

- **Form Accessibility:** Ensure all form inputs have labels, and error messages are clear and associated with the correct input fields.

- **Testing Tools:** Utilize accessibility testing tools like axe, pa11y, or browser extensions to identify and fix issues.

2. Internationalization Testing

Testing for internationalization focuses on verifying that your application works seamlessly in different languages and locales. Here's how you can perform i18n testing:

- **Language Switching:** Test your application with different languages and verify that text translations are correct and fit within UI components.

- **Date and Number Formatting:** Check that dates, numbers, and currencies are correctly formatted according to the selected locale.

- **Right-to-Left (RTL) Languages:** Verify that your application's layout and text alignment adapt correctly for RTL languages like Arabic and Hebrew.

- **Character Encoding:** Test with languages that use different character sets (e.g., Unicode) to ensure proper rendering and handling of special characters.

- **Local Date and Time:** Confirm that the application displays date and time information based on the user's locale.

- **Message Catalog Validation:** Ensure that all messages in your message catalogs are correctly translated and that placeholders are replaced as expected.

- **Edge Cases:** Test for edge cases, such as languages with long words that may cause UI layout issues.

3. Automated Testing

Consider integrating accessibility and i18n testing into your automated testing suite. Tools like Jest, Cypress, and Selenium can be extended with plugins or libraries that support A11y and i18n testing.

4. User Testing

Engage users from different backgrounds and abilities to perform real-world testing. Collect feedback and address issues reported by these users.

5. Continuous Integration

Include A11y and i18n tests in your continuous integration (CI) pipeline to catch issues early in the development process. Automated tests can help maintain accessibility and localization as your application evolves.

6. Documentation

Document your testing procedures and guidelines for developers, testers, and translators. Clear documentation ensures that everyone involved in the project understands and follows best practices.

By incorporating these testing strategies for accessibility and internationalization, you can create a more inclusive and globally accessible TypeScript-based web application. Prioritizing A11y and i18n testing helps you reach a broader audience and ensures a positive user experience for all users, regardless of their abilities or language preferences.

Chapter 18: Security Best Practices

Section 18.1: Common Web Security Threats

Security is of paramount importance in web development. Understanding common web security threats is the first step in protecting your TypeScript applications from potential vulnerabilities. In this section, we'll explore some of the most prevalent web security threats you should be aware of.

1. Injection Attacks

SQL Injection (SQLi): Attackers can inject malicious SQL queries into input fields, exploiting vulnerabilities in your application's database queries. This can lead to unauthorized data access or manipulation.

Cross-Site Scripting (XSS): XSS occurs when untrusted data is included in web pages, enabling attackers to execute malicious scripts in the context of other users' browsers. This can result in data theft or session hijacking.

2. Cross-Site Request Forgery (CSRF)

CSRF attacks trick users into performing actions on a different website unknowingly while authenticated on another site. It can lead to unwanted actions being performed on behalf of the user.

3. Cross-Origin Resource Sharing (CORS)

CORS policies dictate which web domains are allowed to make requests to your web server. Misconfigured CORS settings can expose your application to unauthorized access and data leakage.

4. Authentication and Session Management

Insecure authentication and session management practices can lead to unauthorized access to user accounts. Common issues include weak password policies, session fixation, and storing sensitive data in cookies.

5. Insecure Deserialization

Insecure deserialization occurs when untrusted data is deserialized without proper validation, potentially leading to remote code execution or other security vulnerabilities.

6. Inadequate Input Validation

Failure to validate input data can open doors to various attacks, including injection attacks and buffer overflows. Always validate and sanitize user input to prevent such vulnerabilities.

7. Security Misconfigurations

Improperly configured security settings, such as exposing debug information or leaving sensitive files accessible, can be exploited by attackers. Regularly audit your application's security configurations.

8. Broken Access Control

Inadequate access control can allow unauthorized users to access restricted resources or perform privileged actions. Implement robust access control mechanisms to prevent this.

9. Security Headers

Security headers, like Content Security Policy (CSP) and HTTP Strict Transport Security (HSTS), help protect your application from various attacks. Ensure they are correctly configured.

10. Denial of Service (DoS) and Distributed Denial of Service (DDoS) Attacks

DoS and DDoS attacks aim to overwhelm your application or infrastructure with traffic, causing service disruption. Implement safeguards against these attacks, such as rate limiting and traffic filtering.

11. Security Patch Management

Keep all software and libraries up to date to patch known vulnerabilities. Regularly check for security updates and apply them promptly.

12. Security Education and Training

Educate your development team on secure coding practices and conduct security training to raise awareness about potential threats and how to mitigate them.

Understanding these common web security threats is the first step in building robust and secure TypeScript applications. In the following sections of this chapter, we will delve deeper into secure coding practices and strategies to defend against these threats effectively.

Section 18.2: Secure Coding Practices in TypeScript

Securing your TypeScript applications requires adopting secure coding practices throughout the development process. In this section, we will explore some essential secure coding principles specific to TypeScript.

1. Input Validation and Sanitization

Always validate and sanitize user inputs to prevent injection attacks like SQL injection and XSS. TypeScript's strong typing can help in this regard by ensuring that data types match their expected forms.

```typescript
// Example: Validate and sanitize user input

function sanitizeInput(input: string): string {

// Implement input validation and sanitization logic here

return sanitizedInput;

}
```

2. Use Parameterized Queries

When working with databases, use parameterized queries or prepared statements to prevent SQL injection. Popular libraries like TypeORM provide built-in support for parameterized queries.

```typescript
// Example: Using TypeORM with parameterized query

const username = 'user123';

const query = `SELECT * FROM users WHERE username = $1`;

const result = await connection.query(query, [username]);
```

3. Avoid Eval and Unsafe Reflection

Avoid using eval() and new Function() as they can execute arbitrary code. Similarly, be cautious when using TypeScript's reflection capabilities like Reflect.

```
// Avoid unsafe eval and Function

const userCode = 'console.log("Malicious code here!");';

const unsafeResult = eval(userCode); // Avoid this

// Use safer alternatives

const userFunction = new Function('console.log("Safe code here!");'); // Avoid this

userFunction();
```

4. Authentication and Authorization

Implement secure authentication mechanisms like OAuth and OpenID Connect. Ensure proper authorization checks to prevent unauthorized access to resources.

```
// Example: OAuth authentication in TypeScript

import { OAuth2Client } from 'google-auth-library';

const client = new OAuth2Client(CLIENT_ID);

const ticket = await client.verifyIdToken({ idToken, audience: CLIENT_ID });

const payload = ticket.getPayload();

const userId = payload.sub;
```

5. Prevent Information Leakage

Avoid exposing sensitive information in error messages or debug logs. Use error handling to gracefully handle exceptions without revealing internal details.

```typescript
// Example: Avoid exposing sensitive information

app.get('/profile', (req, res) => {

try {

// Query user profile data

} catch (error) {

console.error('Error:', error.message);

res.status(500).send('Internal Server Error');

}

});
```

6. Use Security Libraries

Leverage security libraries and frameworks like Helmet.js or OWASP's ESAPI for TypeScript to implement security headers, XSS protection, and other security-related features.

```typescript
// Example: Using Helmet.js for security headers

import helmet from 'helmet';

app.use(helmet());
```

7. Data Encryption

Encrypt sensitive data at rest and in transit using strong encryption algorithms. TypeScript has libraries like crypto for implementing encryption and decryption.

```typescript
// Example: Encrypting and decrypting data

import crypto from 'crypto';

const algorithm = 'aes-256-cbc';

const key = crypto.randomBytes(32);

const iv = crypto.randomBytes(16);

const cipher = crypto.createCipheriv(algorithm, key, iv);

const encrypted = cipher.update('Hello, World!', 'utf8', 'hex') + cipher.final('hex');
```

8. Regular Code Audits and Security Scans

Perform regular code audits and security scans of your TypeScript codebase to identify vulnerabilities and potential issues. Tools like ESLint with security plugins can help automate this process.

```
# Example: Running ESLint with security plugins

npm install—save-dev eslint eslint-plugin-security

# Create an ESLint configuration file and include security rules
```

Adopting these secure coding practices in TypeScript will go a long way in ensuring the safety and security of your web applications. Always stay updated on the latest security threats and best practices to protect your software from emerging risks.

Section 18.3: Cross-Site Scripting (XSS) Prevention

Cross-Site Scripting (XSS) is a common web security vulnerability that allows attackers to inject malicious scripts into webpages viewed by other users. Preventing XSS attacks is crucial for securing your TypeScript applications. Here are some strategies to mitigate XSS risks:

1. Input Validation and Output Encoding

Always validate and sanitize user inputs, and encode any data that gets displayed in your web application's HTML. TypeScript's strong typing can help prevent incorrect data types from being used in your templates.

```typescript
// Example: Input validation and output encoding in Angular

import { DomSanitizer } from '@angular/platform-browser';

// Validate and sanitize user input

const userInput = '<script>alert("XSS attack");</script>';

const safeHtml = this.sanitizer.bypassSecurityTrustHtml(userInput);

// Display safe HTML in your template

<div [innerHTML]="safeHtml"></div>
```

2. Content Security Policy (CSP)

Implement a Content Security Policy to control which sources of content are allowed to be executed on your web page. This can help block malicious scripts from executing.

```html
<!--Example: Implementing a Content Security Policy-->

<meta http-equiv="Content-Security-Policy" content="default-src
'self'; script-src 'self' 'unsafe-inline'">
```

3. Use DOM Manipulation Libraries Safely

If your application requires dynamic DOM manipulation, use libraries like Angular, React, or Vue.js, which provide built-in mechanisms to handle data binding and avoid direct manipulation of the DOM.

```javascript
// Example: React component rendering

import React from 'react';

const userMessage = '<script>alert("XSS attack");</script>';

// React will safely render the user message

<div>{userMessage}</div>
```

4. Sanitize HTML

Use libraries like DOMPurify to sanitize and clean user-generated HTML to remove any potentially harmful elements and attributes.

```javascript
// Example: Using DOMPurify to sanitize HTML

import DOMPurify from 'dompurify';

const userInput = '<script>alert("XSS attack");</script>';

const sanitizedHtml = DOMPurify.sanitize(userInput);

<div dangerouslySetInnerHTML={{ __html: sanitizedHtml }}></div>
```

5. Avoid innerHTML

Avoid using innerHTML to inject user-generated content directly into your webpage, as it can introduce XSS vulnerabilities. Instead, use safer mechanisms provided by your framework.

// Example: Avoid using innerHTML

const userInput = '<script>alert("XSS attack");</script>';

// Avoid this:

document.getElementById('elementId').innerHTML = userInput;

// Use a framework-specific method for rendering content safely

6. Keep Dependencies Updated

Regularly update your project dependencies, including libraries and frameworks, to patch known security vulnerabilities. Vulnerabilities in dependencies can be exploited by attackers.

Example: Update project dependencies using npm

npm update

7. Security Testing

Perform regular security testing, including code reviews, static analysis, and dynamic scanning, to identify and remediate XSS vulnerabilities. Tools like ESLint with security plugins can help automate this process.

Example: Running ESLint with security plugins

npm install—save-dev eslint eslint-plugin-security

Create an ESLint configuration file and include security rules

By following these best practices and incorporating security into your development process, you can significantly reduce the risk of XSS attacks in your TypeScript applications. Stay vigilant and keep up to date with the latest security threats and mitigation techniques to maintain the security of your web applications.

Section 18.4: Cross-Site Request Forgery (CSRF) Protection

Cross-Site Request Forgery (CSRF) is a web security vulnerability that occurs when a malicious website tricks a user into performing actions on another site without their knowledge or consent. To protect your TypeScript applications against CSRF attacks, you can implement the following security measures:

1. Use Anti-CSRF Tokens

Implement anti-CSRF tokens to ensure that requests made to your server originate from your own application and not from malicious websites. These tokens are generated on the server and included in forms or API requests. The server validates these tokens before processing requests.

```javascript
// Example: Generating and verifying anti-CSRF tokens in Express.js

const express = require('express');

const csrf = require('csurf');

const bodyParser = require('body-parser');

const app = express();

// Initialize CSRF protection middleware

const csrfProtection = csrf({ cookie: true });
```

```
// Use CSRF protection for specific routes

app.use('/protected', csrfProtection);

app.get('/protected', (req, res) => {

// Include the CSRF token in the response

res.cookie('XSRF-TOKEN', req.csrfToken());

res.render('protected-form');

});

app.post('/protected', (req, res) => {

// Verify the CSRF token before processing the request

if (req.body._csrf === req.csrfToken()) {

// Process the request

// ...

} else {

// Invalid CSRF token

// ...

}

});
```

2. SameSite Cookies

Set the SameSite attribute for your cookies to restrict how cookies are sent in cross-origin requests. Use "Strict" or "Lax" mode to prevent cookies from being sent with unsafe requests.

```
// Example: Setting SameSite attribute for cookies in Express.js

app.use((req, res, next) => {

res.cookie('myCookie', 'myValue', {

sameSite: 'Strict', // or 'Lax'

});

next();

});
```

3. Validate Referrer Header

Check the Referer (referrer) header of incoming requests on your server to ensure that they originate from your own application's domain. Be aware that this header may not be present in all requests.

```
// Example: Validating the Referer header in Express.js

app.use((req, res, next) => {

const referer = req.get('Referer');

if (referer && referer.startsWith('https://your-app-domain.com')) {

// Request is from a trusted source

next();

} else {

// Invalid referrer

res.status(403).send('Forbidden');

}
```

```
});
```

4. Use HTTP Methods Safely

Avoid using HTTP methods for sensitive operations that have side effects (e.g., modifying data) unless the request includes additional verification, such as anti-CSRF tokens.

```
// Example: Use additional verification for sensitive operations

app.post('/delete-account', (req, res) => {

if (req.body._csrf === req.csrfToken()) {

// Verify the CSRF token before deleting the account

// ...

} else {

// Invalid CSRF token

// ...

}

});
```

5. Implement Reauthentication

For critical actions (e.g., changing passwords or email addresses), consider implementing reauthentication, especially for authenticated users who have already logged in. This adds an extra layer of security.

By following these practices, you can reduce the risk of CSRF attacks and enhance the security of your TypeScript web applications. Keep in mind that security is an ongoing process, and it's essential to stay informed about emerging threats and security best practices to protect your application effectively.

Section 18.5: Security Auditing and Vulnerability Scanning

Ensuring the security of your TypeScript applications is an ongoing process. To help identify vulnerabilities and maintain a secure codebase, consider implementing security auditing and vulnerability scanning practices. These practices can help you proactively address potential security issues before they become significant problems.

1. Code Reviews

Regular code reviews with a focus on security can be an effective way to identify and fix security vulnerabilities in your TypeScript code. Establish a process for peer reviews, where team members can assess each other's code for security flaws, adherence to security best practices, and potential vulnerabilities.

Consider using automated code analysis tools like ESLint with security-related plugins, such as eslint-plugin-security, to catch common security issues during the code review process.

2. Penetration Testing

Penetration testing, often referred to as "pen testing," involves simulating real-world attacks on your application to identify weaknesses and vulnerabilities. Hire or consult with security experts who can perform penetration testing to assess your TypeScript application's security posture.

These experts will attempt to exploit vulnerabilities and provide you with a detailed report of their findings, allowing you to remediate the issues promptly.

3. Dependency Scanning

Regularly scan your application's dependencies for known security vulnerabilities. Use tools like OWASP Dependency-Check or commercial solutions that can automatically analyze your project's dependencies and identify any components with known vulnerabilities.

4. Security Headers

Utilize security headers in your TypeScript application to enhance its security. Headers like Content Security Policy (CSP), Strict-Transport-Security (HSTS), and X-Content-Type-Options can help protect against common web vulnerabilities like XSS (Cross-Site Scripting) and data injection attacks.

Here's an example of setting up CSP headers in an Express.js application:

```
const helmet = require('helmet');

app.use(helmet.contentSecurityPolicy({

directives: {

defaultSrc: ["'self'"],

scriptSrc: ["'self'", 'trusted-cdn.com'],

// Add more directives as needed

},
```

```
}));
```

5. Security Patch Management

Stay informed about security patches and updates for the software libraries, frameworks, and packages you use in your TypeScript project. Vulnerabilities in third-party dependencies can affect the security of your application. Regularly update your dependencies to their latest secure versions.

6. Security Training and Awareness

Invest in security training and awareness programs for your development team. Educate your developers about common security threats and best practices. Encourage a security-conscious culture where everyone takes responsibility for the security of the application.

7. Continuous Monitoring

Implement continuous monitoring practices to detect and respond to security incidents promptly. Use security monitoring tools and services to monitor your application's behavior, traffic patterns, and potential security breaches.

8. Compliance and Regulations

If your TypeScript application processes sensitive data or is subject to specific regulations (e.g., GDPR, HIPAA), ensure that your application complies with the necessary security and privacy requirements. Consult legal and compliance experts if needed.

By incorporating these security auditing and vulnerability scanning practices into your TypeScript development workflow, you can strengthen the security of your applications and reduce the risk of security breaches and data leaks. Security should be an integral part of your development process, not just an afterthought.

Chapter 19: Beyond the Browser: TypeScript in Node.js

Section 19.1: TypeScript for Server-Side Development

Node.js is a runtime environment that allows you to execute JavaScript on the server side. With TypeScript, you can bring the benefits of strong typing, interfaces, and modern JavaScript features to your server-side code. This section explores how TypeScript can be used for server-side development with Node.js.

1. Setting Up a TypeScript Node.js Project

To get started with TypeScript in a Node.js project, you'll need to set up your development environment. Here are the steps:

1.1. Initialize a New Node.js Project

If you haven't already, create a new directory for your project and run the following command to initialize a new Node.js project:

npm init -y

1.2. Install TypeScript

Install TypeScript as a development dependency:

npm install typescript—save-dev

416

1.3. Create a TypeScript Configuration File

Generate a tsconfig.json file to configure TypeScript in your project:

npx tsc—init

You can customize this file to suit your project's needs.

1.4. Create a TypeScript File

Create a TypeScript file (e.g., index.ts) where you'll write your server-side code. You can use modern JavaScript features and TypeScript-specific syntax.

2. Building and Running the TypeScript Application

After writing your TypeScript code, you need to compile it to JavaScript before running it with Node.js. Here's how:

2.1. Compile TypeScript to JavaScript

Compile your TypeScript code using the TypeScript compiler (tsc):

npx tsc

This command will generate JavaScript files based on your TypeScript code and configuration.

2.2. Run the Node.js Application

You can now run your Node.js application using the node command:

node dist/index.js

Replace dist/index.js with the path to your compiled JavaScript file.

3. Leveraging TypeScript Features

By using TypeScript in your Node.js project, you can take advantage of several features:

3.1. Strong Typing

TypeScript allows you to define types for variables, function parameters, and return values, making your code more robust and less error-prone.

```
function add(a: number, b: number): number {

return a + b;

}
```

3.2. Interfaces and Custom Types

You can define interfaces and custom types to represent complex data structures and ensure consistency in your code.

```
interface User {

id: number;

name: string;

}

const user: User = {

id: 1,

name: 'John Doe',
```

```
};
```

3.3. Modern JavaScript Features

TypeScript supports modern JavaScript features like async/await, destructuring, and modules, allowing you to write clean and maintainable code.

```
import { readFile } from 'fs/promises';

async function readData() {

const data = await readFile('data.txt', 'utf-8');

console.log(data);

}
```

4. Popular Node.js Frameworks with TypeScript

Many Node.js frameworks and libraries offer TypeScript support, making it easier to build server-side applications. Some popular options include:

- Express.js with TypeScript: A widely-used web application framework.

- NestJS: A progressive Node.js framework for building efficient, scalable, and maintainable server-side applications.

- TypeORM: An Object-Relational Mapping (ORM) library for TypeScript and JavaScript.

In this section, we've explored the basics of using TypeScript for server-side development in Node.js. With TypeScript's strong typing and modern JavaScript features, you can build robust and maintainable server applications.

Section 19.2: Building RESTful APIs with TypeScript

In this section, we'll delve into building RESTful APIs using TypeScript and Node.js. RESTful APIs are a common way to expose your server's functionality to clients, whether they are web applications, mobile apps, or other services. TypeScript can be a powerful tool for creating and maintaining APIs due to its strong typing and code organization features.

1. Setting Up a TypeScript API Project

Before we start building our RESTful API, we need to set up our project:

1.1. Initialize a New Node.js Project

If you haven't already, create a new directory for your project and run the following command to initialize a new Node.js project:

npm init -y

1.2. Install Dependencies

You'll need some dependencies for building a RESTful API:

- **Express.js**: A popular web application framework for Node.js.

- **Body-parser**: Middleware for parsing incoming request bodies.

- **Mongoose**: An Object Data Modeling (ODM) library for MongoDB.

Install these dependencies with the following command:

npm install express body-parser mongoose

1.3. Install TypeScript

Install TypeScript as a development dependency:

npm install typescript—save-dev

1.4. Create a TypeScript Configuration File

Generate a tsconfig.json file to configure TypeScript in your project:

npx tsc—init

2. Creating a Simple RESTful API

Let's create a basic RESTful API that manages a list of items. Here's a step-by-step guide:

2.1. Create a TypeScript File

Create a TypeScript file (e.g., app.ts) and start by importing the necessary modules:

import express, { Request, Response } **from** 'express';

import bodyParser **from** 'body-parser';

import mongoose **from** 'mongoose';

2.2. Initialize Express

Initialize Express and configure middleware:

const app = express();

app.use(bodyParser.json());

2.3. Define the Item Model

Define the data structure of an item using Mongoose:

const itemSchema = **new** mongoose.Schema({

name: String,

description: String,

});

const Item = mongoose.model('Item', itemSchema);

2.4. Create API Endpoints

Create API endpoints for managing items:

// Get all items

app.get('/api/items', **async** (req: Request, res: Response) => {

const items = **await** Item.find();

res.json(items);

});

// Create a new item

```typescript
app.post('/api/items', async (req: Request, res: Response) => {

const newItem = new Item(req.body);

await newItem.save();

res.status(201).json(newItem);

});

// Get a single item by ID

app.get('/api/items/:id', async (req: Request, res: Response) => {

const item = await Item.findById(req.params.id);

if (!item) {

return res.status(404).json({ message: 'Item not found' });

}

res.json(item);

});

// Update an item by ID

app.put('/api/items/:id', async (req: Request, res: Response) => {

const item = await Item.findByIdAndUpdate(req.params.id,
req.body, { new: true });

if (!item) {

return res.status(404).json({ message: 'Item not found' });

}

res.json(item);
```

```
});

// Delete an item by ID

app.delete('/api/items/:id', async (req: Request, res: Response) => {

const item = await Item.findByIdAndRemove(req.params.id);

if (!item) {

return res.status(404).json({ message: 'Item not found' });

}

res.json({ message: 'Item deleted' });

});
```

2.5. Connect to MongoDB

Connect to your MongoDB database:

```
mongoose.connect('mongodb://localhost:27017/mydb', {

useNewUrlParser: true,

useUnifiedTopology: true,

});
```

2.6. Start the Express Server

Start the Express server:

```
const PORT = process.env.PORT || 3000;

app.listen(PORT, () => {
```

```
console.log(`Server is running on port ${PORT}`);

});
```

3. Testing the API

You can use tools like Postman[1] or curl[2] to test your API endpoints. Here's an example of using curl to create a new item:

```
curl -X POST -H "Content-Type: application/json" -d '{"name": "Item 1", "description": "Description of Item 1"}' http://localhost:3000/api/items
```

This command sends a POST request to your API to create a new item.

In this section, we've created a basic RESTful API using TypeScript and Express.js. You can extend and customize this API to suit your specific application needs. TypeScript's strong typing and modern

Section 19.3: Database Access with TypeScript

In this section, we'll explore how to work with databases using TypeScript, specifically focusing on MongoDB as an example. Databases are crucial for storing and managing the data that your applications rely on, and TypeScript can help ensure type safety and maintainability when interacting with databases.

1. Setting Up MongoDB

Before we dive into TypeScript database access, make sure you have MongoDB installed and running locally or have access to a remote

---

1. https://www.postman.com/

2. https://curl.se/

MongoDB instance. You can download and install MongoDB from the official website[3].

2. Installing Dependencies

We'll need some libraries to work with MongoDB and TypeScript. Let's install them as project dependencies:

npm install mongoose @types/mongoose

- **mongoose**: Mongoose is an Object Data Modeling (ODM) library for MongoDB that provides an easy-to-use interface for interacting with MongoDB.

- **@types/mongoose**: This package provides TypeScript type definitions for Mongoose.

3. Creating a Database Connection

In your TypeScript project, create a TypeScript file (e.g., db.ts) for managing the database connection. Here's an example of how to set up a connection to MongoDB using Mongoose:

import mongoose **from** 'mongoose';

// MongoDB connection URL (change this to your database URL)

const DB_URL = 'mongodb://localhost:27017/mydb';

mongoose

.connect(DB_URL, {

useNewUrlParser: **true**,

useUnifiedTopology: **true**,

```
})
.then(() => {

console.log('Connected to MongoDB');

})

.catch((error) => {

console.error('MongoDB connection error:', error);

});

// Create a MongoDB connection instance

const db = mongoose.connection;

// Handle MongoDB connection events

db.on('error', console.error.bind(console, 'MongoDB connection
error:'));

db.once('open', () => {

console.log('MongoDB connected successfully');

});
```

Make sure to replace DB_URL with the URL of your MongoDB database. This code establishes a connection to the database and handles connection events.

4. Creating Mongoose Models

Mongoose models define the structure of the documents that will be stored in the MongoDB collection. Here's an example of creating a Mongoose model for a User:

```typescript
import mongoose, { Schema, Document } from 'mongoose';

// Define the user schema

const userSchema = new Schema({

username: { type: String, required: true },

email: { type: String, required: true },

age: { type: Number },

});

// Define the user interface (optional but recommended for type safety)

interface IUser extends Document {

username: string;

email: string;

age?: number;

}

// Create the User model

const User = mongoose.model<IUser>('User', userSchema);

export default User;
```

In this example, we define the schema for a user document and create a Mongoose model called User.

5. CRUD Operations

With the database connection and model in place, you can perform CRUD (Create, Read, Update, Delete) operations on the database. Here are some examples:

5.1. Creating a User

```
const newUser = new User({

username: 'john_doe',

email: 'john@example.com',

age: 30,

});

newUser.save()

.then((user) => {

console.log('User created:', user);

})

.catch((error) => {

console.error('Error creating user:', error);

});
```

5.2. Reading Users

```
User.find()

.then((users) => {
```

```javascript
console.log('Users:', users);

})

.catch((error) => {

console.error('Error fetching users:', error);

});
```

5.3. Updating a User

```javascript
User.findByIdAndUpdate(userId, { age: 31 }, { new: true })

.then((user) => {

console.log('Updated user:', user);

})

.catch((error) => {

console.error('Error updating user:', error);

});
```

5.4. Deleting a User

```javascript
User.findByIdAndDelete(userId)

.then(() => {

console.log('User deleted');

})

.catch((error) => {
```

```
console.error('Error deleting user:', error);
```

```
});
```

These are just basic examples of working with MongoDB using TypeScript and Mongoose. You can expand upon these to build more complex database interactions in your applications.

6. TypeScript Typing

TypeScript provides strong typing for Mongoose models. When you define an interface for your documents, you can take advantage of type checking and auto-completion in your code. This helps catch type-related errors at compile-time rather than runtime.

By following these steps, you can effectively use TypeScript with MongoDB to create, retrieve

Section 19.4: Testing and Debugging Node.js Apps with TypeScript

In this section, we will explore testing and debugging techniques for Node.js applications written in TypeScript. Robust testing and effective debugging are essential for ensuring the reliability and maintainability of your Node.js projects.

1. Testing Node.js Applications

1.1. Test Frameworks

There are several popular test frameworks available for Node.js applications written in TypeScript. Some commonly used ones include:

- **Jest**: A popular and highly extensible test framework that works well with TypeScript. It provides a rich set of features, including mocking, assertions, and parallel test execution.

- **Mocha**: A versatile test framework that can be used with various assertion libraries like Chai. It's known for its flexibility and extensibility.

- **Jasmine**: A behavior-driven development (BDD) framework for testing JavaScript and TypeScript code. It provides a readable syntax for defining tests.

1.2. Writing Tests

When writing tests for TypeScript applications, you should use TypeScript's type system to ensure type safety in your tests. Here's an example using Jest:

```typescript
import { sum } from './math'; // Import the function to be tested

describe('sum function', () => {

it('should add two numbers correctly', () => {

expect(sum(1, 2)).toBe(3);

expect(sum(-1, 1)).toBe(0);

expect(sum(0, 0)).toBe(0);

});

it('should handle edge cases', () => {

expect(sum(1, -1)).toBe(0);
```

```
expect(sum(100, -100)).toBe(0);

});

});
```

In this example, we import the sum function from a module and write test cases using Jest's describe and it functions. Jest provides the expect function for making assertions.

1.3. Running Tests

To run your tests, use the test runner associated with your chosen test framework. For Jest, you can run tests with the following command:

```
npx jest
```

1.4. Mocking Dependencies

When testing modules with external dependencies (e.g., a database or API calls), you may want to mock these dependencies to isolate the code you're testing. Jest provides mocking capabilities for this purpose. For instance, you can use jest.mock to replace a module's implementation with a mock implementation.

2. Debugging Node.js Applications

2.1. Debugging Tools

Debugging TypeScript Node.js applications can be done using various tools, including:

• **Node.js Inspector**: This built-in debugging tool allows you to debug your TypeScript code by setting breakpoints and inspecting variables.

• **VS Code Debugger**: If you're using Visual Studio Code (VS Code), it provides a powerful debugging experience. You can set breakpoints, step through code, and inspect variables directly from the editor.

2.2. Configuring Debugging in VS Code

To debug a TypeScript Node.js application in VS Code, follow these steps:

1. Create a launch configuration in your project's .vscode/launch.json file.

```json
{

"version": "0.2.0",

"configurations": [

{

"name": "Debug TypeScript",

"type": "node",

"request": "launch",

"program": "${workspaceFolder}/src/index.ts",

"outFiles": ["${workspaceFolder}/dist/**/*.js"],

"sourceMaps": true,
```

```
"skipFiles": ["<node_internals>/**"]

}

]

}
```

In this example, "program" should point to your TypeScript entry file (e.g., index.ts), "outFiles" should include the path to your compiled JavaScript files, and "sourceMaps" should be set to true to enable source map support.

1. Set breakpoints in your TypeScript code by clicking in the left margin of the editor.
2. Start debugging by selecting the configuration you created and clicking the "Run and Debug" button in VS Code.

2.3. Debugging with Node.js Inspector

To debug your TypeScript Node.js application using Node.js Inspector, you can start your application with the —inspect flag:

```
node—inspect dist/index.js
```

This will start the Node.js Inspector server, and you can connect to it using tools like Chrome DevTools or Visual Studio Code.

3. Continuous Integration (CI) and Testing

To ensure that your tests run consistently and automatically on every code change or pull request, consider integrating a CI/CD (Continuous Integration/Continuous Deployment) system into your development workflow. Popular CI/CD platforms include Jenkins, Travis CI, CircleCI, and GitHub Actions.

By setting up CI, you can automatically run your test suite on each code push and catch issues early in the development process.

In this section, we've explored testing and debugging techniques for Node.js applications written in TypeScript. Testing and debugging are crucial aspects of building reliable and maintainable applications, and these practices help identify and resolve issues efficiently. Combining testing with continuous integration can further streamline your development workflow and enhance code quality.

Section 19.5: Serverless Functions with TypeScript

Serverless computing has gained popularity as a scalable and cost-effective way to deploy applications. In this section, we'll explore how to create serverless functions using TypeScript and deploy them on serverless platforms like AWS Lambda, Azure Functions, or Google Cloud Functions.

1. Serverless Basics

Serverless computing, often referred to as Function as a Service (FaaS), allows you to run individual functions or microservices in the cloud without managing the underlying infrastructure. Some key benefits of serverless include:

- **Scalability**: Serverless platforms automatically scale your functions in response to traffic, ensuring high availability and performance.

- **Cost-Efficiency**: You only pay for the compute resources used during function execution, making it cost-effective for many workloads.

- **Reduced Management**: Serverless providers handle server provisioning, maintenance, and scaling, allowing developers to focus on code.

2. Writing Serverless Functions in TypeScript

To create serverless functions with TypeScript, follow these general steps:

2.1. Set Up Your Development Environment

Ensure you have Node.js and npm (Node Package Manager) installed. Initialize a new TypeScript project and install the required dependencies:

npm init -y

npm install typescript @types/node

2.2. Create a TypeScript Function

Write your serverless function in TypeScript. For example, here's a simple AWS Lambda function that responds to an HTTP request using the AWS Lambda and AWS API Gateway SDKs:

```typescript
import { APIGatewayEvent, APIGatewayProxyResult } from 'aws-lambda';

export const handler = async (

event: APIGatewayEvent

): Promise<APIGatewayProxyResult> => {

try {
```

```
// Your function logic here

const response = {

statusCode: 200,

body: JSON.stringify({ message: 'Hello, Serverless World!' }),

};

return response;

} catch (error) {

return {

statusCode: 500,

body: JSON.stringify({ error: 'Internal Server Error' }),

};

}

};
```

2.3. Build and Package

Compile your TypeScript code into JavaScript using the TypeScript compiler (tsc). Additionally, create a deployment package that includes your compiled JavaScript files and any dependencies. For AWS Lambda, you would typically package your code in a zip file.

2.4. Deploy to a Serverless Platform

Each serverless platform has its deployment process. For AWS Lambda, you can use the AWS Command Line Interface (CLI) or services like AWS SAM (Serverless Application Model) for more complex deployments.

2.5. Configure Triggers

Serverless functions can be triggered by various events, such as HTTP requests, database changes, or scheduled tasks. Configure the triggers based on your application's requirements.

3. Serverless Frameworks

To simplify serverless development with TypeScript, consider using serverless frameworks like the Serverless Framework or AWS SAM. These frameworks provide templates, deployment automation, and tools for managing serverless applications.

4. Monitoring and Debugging

Serverless platforms offer monitoring and debugging tools to help you troubleshoot and optimize your functions. Utilize these tools to gain insights into function performance and diagnose issues.

5. Conclusion

Serverless functions with TypeScript offer a flexible and efficient way to build and deploy scalable applications. By following best practices and leveraging serverless frameworks, you can streamline the development and deployment process, making it easier to focus on building your application's logic.

Chapter 20: The Future of TypeScript

Section 20.1: TypeScript and ECMAScript Standards

TypeScript is closely related to the ECMAScript (ES) standards, which define the scripting language features supported by web browsers and other JavaScript environments. This section explores TypeScript's relationship with ES standards and how TypeScript evolves alongside them.

1. TypeScript and ECMAScript Compatibility

TypeScript is a superset of JavaScript and adheres to the ECMAScript standards. This means that any valid JavaScript code is also valid TypeScript code. TypeScript introduces additional features like static typing and interfaces, but it doesn't break compatibility with JavaScript.

When working with TypeScript, you can choose the target ECMAScript version to compile your code into. This allows you to leverage the latest ES features while ensuring compatibility with specific JavaScript environments. For example, you can target ES5 for broader browser support or ES2022 for the latest language features.

2. Proposal Process

The ECMAScript standards evolve through a proposal process governed by the TC39 committee. TypeScript actively participates in this process, and its developers contribute to ECMAScript proposals. This collaboration ensures that TypeScript can adopt upcoming JavaScript features as they become part of the standard.

3. Features Ahead of the Curve

TypeScript often introduces experimental features that may eventually become part of the ECMAScript standard. Developers can enable these features by configuring the TypeScript compiler to allow experimental options. This enables early adoption of proposed features while providing valuable feedback to the TC39 committee.

4. Declaration Files for Existing Libraries

TypeScript provides a rich ecosystem of declaration files (.d.ts) that describe the type signatures of existing JavaScript libraries. These declaration files enable TypeScript developers to work with popular libraries while benefiting from type checking. The DefinitelyTyped repository hosts thousands of community-contributed declaration files.

5. TypeScript's Impact on JavaScript

TypeScript's popularity and developer tooling have influenced the JavaScript ecosystem. Features like static typing and code analysis, initially introduced by TypeScript, have been adopted by JavaScript itself. Tools like Babel, which transpile modern JavaScript into older versions, are inspired by TypeScript's approach to language evolution.

6. Conclusion

TypeScript's alignment with ECMAScript standards and its active involvement in the proposal process make it a forward-looking language. Developers can confidently use TypeScript to write modern JavaScript code while benefiting from strong typing, tooling, and a smooth transition to future ECMAScript versions.

As JavaScript continues to evolve, TypeScript remains a valuable companion for web development.

Section 20.2: Emerging Trends in Web Development

Web development is a dynamic field, and staying up-to-date with emerging trends is crucial for developers. In this section, we'll explore some of the current and future trends in web development and how TypeScript fits into this ever-evolving landscape.

1. Progressive Web Apps (PWAs)

Progressive Web Apps (PWAs) continue to gain momentum in the web development world. PWAs offer a more engaging and app-like experience for users, including features like offline access, push notifications, and smooth performance. TypeScript's strong typing and tooling support can aid in building robust PWAs, ensuring code quality and reliability.

2. Serverless Architecture

Serverless computing is changing the way web applications are developed and deployed. With serverless platforms like AWS Lambda, Azure Functions, and Google Cloud Functions, developers can focus on writing code while the cloud provider manages infrastructure. TypeScript's static typing can help catch errors early and provide confidence in serverless applications.

3. Jamstack Architecture

Jamstack (JavaScript, APIs, and Markup) is a modern architecture for building web applications. It emphasizes decoupling the front end from the back end and using APIs for dynamic functionality.

TypeScript's type safety is valuable when working with APIs, ensuring that data structures are correctly defined and used.

4. WebAssembly (Wasm)

WebAssembly is a low-level binary instruction format that runs in web browsers at near-native speed. It enables running code written in languages like C, C++, and Rust on the web. While TypeScript itself doesn't compile to WebAssembly, it can be used alongside WebAssembly projects to provide type checking and tooling support for interfacing with WebAssembly modules.

5. Single Page Applications (SPAs)

SPAs remain a popular choice for building web applications due to their fast and responsive user experiences. TypeScript's static typing is particularly beneficial in large SPAs, where complex data flows and component interactions need to be well-defined.

6. Micro Frontends

Micro frontends are an architectural approach that extends the microservices concept to the front end. They involve breaking down a web application into smaller, independently developed and deployable parts. TypeScript's module system and type safety can help manage the complexity of micro frontend architectures.

7. Web3 and Blockchain

As blockchain technology and decentralized applications (dApps) gain traction, web developers are exploring ways to integrate blockchain into web applications. TypeScript's strong typing and tooling support can assist in building reliable and secure interfaces for interacting with blockchain networks.

8. Conclusion

Web development is an ever-evolving field, and TypeScript's versatility and developer-friendly features position it well for adapting to emerging trends. By staying informed about new technologies and trends, TypeScript developers can leverage their skills to build cutting-edge web applications that meet the evolving needs of users and businesses.

Section 20.3: TypeScript and WebAssembly

WebAssembly, often abbreviated as Wasm, is a binary instruction format designed to run at near-native speed in web browsers. It opens up new possibilities for web development by allowing you to compile code from languages like C, C++, Rust, and more into a format that can be executed in the browser alongside JavaScript. In this section, we'll explore the relationship between TypeScript and WebAssembly and how they can be used together.

WebAssembly and TypeScript

WebAssembly and TypeScript are not directly related in terms of their goals, but they can complement each other in web development projects. TypeScript is a statically-typed superset of JavaScript that offers type safety and developer-friendly features, while WebAssembly provides high-performance execution of low-level code.

Here are some scenarios where TypeScript and WebAssembly can work together:

1. **Using WebAssembly Modules**: TypeScript can interact with WebAssembly modules by providing type definitions for functions and data structures exposed by the modules.

This helps ensure type safety when calling WebAssembly functions from TypeScript code.

2. **Compiling TypeScript to WebAssembly**: While TypeScript primarily compiles to JavaScript, you can explore tools and projects that compile TypeScript directly to WebAssembly. This approach can be valuable for specific use cases where high performance and low-level control are essential.

Benefits of Using TypeScript with WebAssembly

1. **Type Safety**: TypeScript's static type system can help catch type-related errors at compile time, reducing the chances of runtime errors when interacting with WebAssembly.
2. **Tooling Support**: TypeScript's robust tooling, including editors like Visual Studio Code, offers intelligent code completion, type checking, and debugging support when working with WebAssembly.
3. **Documentation and IntelliSense**: TypeScript's type definitions provide rich documentation and IntelliSense support, making it easier to understand and use WebAssembly modules in your code.

Example: Using TypeScript with a WebAssembly Module

Suppose you have a WebAssembly module that calculates mathematical operations. You can create TypeScript type definitions for the module's functions:

```
// wasm-module.d.ts
```

```
declare module 'math-wasm' {
```

```
export function add(a: number, b: number): number;

export function subtract(a: number, b: number): number;

}
```

Then, in your TypeScript code, you can import and use the WebAssembly functions with type safety:

```
import { add, subtract } from 'math-wasm';

const result1 = add(5, 3); // Type-checked addition

const result2 = subtract(8, 2); // Type-checked subtraction
```

Conclusion

WebAssembly and TypeScript are powerful technologies that can be used together to build efficient and type-safe web applications. While not all projects may require the use of WebAssembly, having the flexibility to integrate it into your TypeScript projects can provide significant performance benefits, especially for compute-intensive tasks. As the web development landscape continues to evolve, understanding how these technologies complement each other can be a valuable asset for developers.

ASSISTANT

Section 20.3: TypeScript and WebAssembly

WebAssembly (Wasm) is a binary instruction format designed for web browsers, enabling the execution of high-performance code written in languages like C, C++, Rust, and more. It allows web applications to run at near-native speed, opening up new possibilities for web development. In this section, we'll explore the integration of TypeScript with WebAssembly and how they work together to create powerful web applications.

WebAssembly and Its Benefits

WebAssembly is designed to run efficiently on web browsers, providing benefits like:

1. **Near-Native Performance**: WebAssembly code executes at near-native speed, making it suitable for compute-intensive tasks and graphics-heavy applications.
2. **Cross-Browser Compatibility**: WebAssembly is supported by all major browsers, ensuring broad compatibility.
3. **Safety and Security**: WebAssembly's sandboxed execution environment enhances security by isolating code from the host system.
4. **Language Agnostic**: WebAssembly is language-agnostic, meaning you can use languages other than JavaScript to write web applications.

Integrating TypeScript with WebAssembly

While TypeScript itself doesn't compile directly to WebAssembly, you can use TypeScript in conjunction with languages that do, like Rust or AssemblyScript. Here's how the integration typically works:

1. **Write WebAssembly Code**: You write the core logic of your application in a language like Rust or AssemblyScript. These languages have WebAssembly as one of their compilation targets.
2. **TypeScript for WebAssembly Interface**: You use TypeScript to define the interface between your JavaScript/TypeScript code and the WebAssembly module.

This involves specifying function signatures, data structures, and their types.

3. **Compile WebAssembly**: You compile the code written in Rust or AssemblyScript into a WebAssembly binary file (usually with a .wasm extension). This file contains the low-level instructions for the browser to execute.

4. **Import WebAssembly Module**: In your TypeScript/JavaScript code, you import the compiled WebAssembly module and use the TypeScript-defined interface to interact with it. TypeScript's type checking helps ensure that you're using the module correctly.

Example Use Cases

Here are some use cases where TypeScript and WebAssembly can be a powerful combination:

- **Graphics and Gaming**: Building 2D or 3D games and graphics-intensive applications with high-performance requirements.

- **Scientific Computing**: Performing complex scientific calculations in the browser efficiently.

- **Data Processing**: Handling large datasets and performing data processing tasks with speed.

TypeScript and WebAssembly Tooling

Several tools and libraries support TypeScript and WebAssembly integration:

- **AssemblyScript**: A TypeScript-like language that compiles to WebAssembly. It simplifies the process of writing WebAssembly modules with TypeScript-like syntax.

- **wasm-bindgen**: A Rust library that generates TypeScript/JavaScript bindings for WebAssembly modules written in Rust. It eases the interaction between TypeScript and Rust-based WebAssembly.

- **WebAssembly Studio**: An online IDE for building WebAssembly applications that offers TypeScript integration.

Conclusion

WebAssembly is a game-changer in web development, providing performance and versatility. By combining TypeScript's type safety and tooling support with WebAssembly's execution speed, developers can create web applications that deliver impressive user experiences while meeting high-performance demands. Learning to work with these technologies can open up exciting opportunities in the world of web development.

Section 20.4: Progressive Enhancement with TypeScript

Progressive enhancement is an important concept in web development that focuses on delivering a basic, functional experience to all users and then progressively enhancing that experience for users with more capable devices or browsers. TypeScript can play a significant role in achieving progressive enhancement by providing a foundation for building robust and accessible web applications.

Core Principles of Progressive Enhancement

Before we delve into how TypeScript fits into progressive enhancement, let's recap the core principles:

1. **Baseline Functionality**: Start with the essential functionality that works across all devices and browsers. This ensures that everyone, regardless of their device or browser, can access your content.
2. **Enhancement for Modern Browsers**: Once the baseline functionality is in place, enhance the user experience for users with modern browsers or devices by adding extra features, improved performance, and interactivity.
3. **Graceful Degradation**: Ensure that if a user's browser or device doesn't support certain enhancements, the website gracefully degrades to the baseline functionality without breaking.
4. **Accessibility**: Make your web application accessible to all users, including those with disabilities. Accessibility is a core part of progressive enhancement.

TypeScript's Role in Progressive Enhancement

TypeScript contributes to progressive enhancement in several ways:

1. **Type Safety**: TypeScript enforces type safety in your codebase, reducing the likelihood of runtime errors. This means the baseline functionality is less prone to bugs.
2. **Enhanced Developer Productivity**: TypeScript's rich tooling and features, such as code completion and type checking, improve developer productivity when adding enhancements.
3. **Maintainability**: As your codebase grows, TypeScript helps maintain code quality, making it easier to add new

features and enhancements.

4. **Accessibility**: TypeScript can be used to build accessible components and features, ensuring that enhancements are usable by all.

Practical Implementation

To implement progressive enhancement with TypeScript:

1. **Identify Baseline Functionality**: Determine the core functionality that should work without any enhancements. Write TypeScript code to implement this functionality.
2. **Enhance User Experience**: Use TypeScript to add enhancements for modern browsers. This might include adding interactive features, animations, or optimizations for performance.
3. **Graceful Degradation**: Ensure that if a user's browser lacks support for enhancements, the baseline functionality is still usable without errors. TypeScript's type system helps catch issues during development.
4. **Accessibility**: Throughout the development process, pay attention to accessibility. Use TypeScript to create accessible components and features, and test them with assistive technologies.

TypeScript and Feature Detection

TypeScript can work hand-in-hand with feature detection techniques to determine whether certain enhancements should be applied. For example, you can use TypeScript to check for the availability of certain browser APIs or features before attempting to use them.

// TypeScript feature detection example

```typescript
if ('serviceWorker' in navigator) {

// Use Service Worker for enhanced offline capabilities

navigator.serviceWorker.register('/sw.js');

} else {

// Provide a fallback for browsers that don't support Service Workers

// (e.g., older browsers)

}
```

Conclusion

Progressive enhancement is a web development approach that ensures inclusivity, performance, and a better user experience for all users. TypeScript can be a valuable tool in implementing progressive enhancement by providing type safety, enhancing developer productivity, and enabling maintainable and accessible code. When used in conjunction with feature detection, TypeScript helps ensure that enhancements are applied where appropriate, without compromising the baseline functionality.

Section 20.5: Keeping Up with TypeScript Updates

TypeScript is an evolving language, and it receives regular updates and improvements. To stay current and make the most of TypeScript's features and capabilities, it's crucial to keep up with these updates and integrate them into your projects. In this section, we'll discuss strategies for staying informed about TypeScript updates and how to update your existing projects effectively.

1. Official TypeScript Website

The official TypeScript website (https://www.typescriptlang.org) is your primary source for TypeScript updates. It provides release notes for each new version, including details about new features, bug fixes, and breaking changes. Regularly checking the website can help you stay informed about the latest developments.

2. TypeScript Release Notes

As mentioned earlier, the TypeScript release notes are published on the official website. These notes provide a comprehensive overview of changes in each version. When a new TypeScript version is released, it's a good practice to review the release notes to understand what has been introduced or modified.

3. TypeScript's npm Package

TypeScript is distributed as an npm package. You can check for updates by running the following command in your project directory:

```
npm outdated typescript
```

This command will show you the currently installed version and the latest version available on npm. If there's a newer version, you can update your project by running:

```
npm update typescript
```

4. Visual Studio Code Integration

If you use Visual Studio Code as your code editor, it has excellent TypeScript support built in. It can automatically detect TypeScript updates and provide you with notifications and prompts to update your project's TypeScript version.

5. Community and Forums

The TypeScript community is active and engaged. Platforms like Stack Overflow and the TypeScript subreddit (r/typescript) are great places to ask questions and get updates from other developers. You can also participate in discussions about TypeScript's future development.

Updating Your TypeScript Projects

When a new TypeScript version is released, updating your projects is essential to benefit from new features and improvements while maintaining compatibility. Here's a general process for updating:

1. **Review Release Notes**: Read the release notes for the new TypeScript version to understand what has changed. Pay attention to any breaking changes or deprecations that may affect your code.
2. **Update TypeScript Globally**: If you want to update TypeScript globally (for all projects), you can use the following command:

```
npm install -g typescript@latest
```

1. **Update Project's TypeScript Version**: For individual projects, update the TypeScript version in your project's package.json file:

```
"devDependencies": {

"typescript": "^4.5.2"
```

```
}
```

Then, run npm install to update the TypeScript version in your project.

1. **Review and Fix Errors**: After updating, review your project for any TypeScript errors or warnings. Address them based on the information provided in the release notes.
2. **Update Typings**: If you use TypeScript typings (e.g., @types packages) for external libraries, ensure they are compatible with the new TypeScript version and update them if necessary.
3. **Test Thoroughly**: After updating, thoroughly test your application to ensure that everything works as expected. Pay special attention to any code that might be affected by breaking changes.
4. **Commit Changes**: Once you've updated and tested your project, commit the changes to your version control system.

By following these steps, you can effectively keep your TypeScript projects up to date and take advantage of the latest features and improvements while ensuring the stability and maintainability of your codebase.

www.ingramcontent.com/pod-product-compliance
Lightning Source LLC
Chambersburg PA
CBHW061418150726
47987CB00001B/14